To Charlie
with regards
Bill

Electronic Information Processing

Physical Principles and Materials Technology

MODERN FRONTIERS IN APPLIED SCIENCE

Noise Performance Factors in Communication Systems
by W.W. Mumford and E.H. Scheibe

Laser Applications
by W.V. Smith

The Microwave Engineer's Handbook
by Ted Saad

Logarithmic Video Amplifiers
by R.S. Hughes

Parallel Coupled Lines and Directional Couplers
by Dr. Leo Young

Microwave Filters Using Parallel Coupled Lines
by Dr. Leo Young

Data Modem Selection and Evaluation Guide
by V.V. Vilips

Design, Performance and Application of Microwave
Semiconductor Control Components
by Kenneth E. Mortenson and Jose M. Borrego

Adaptive Electronics
by Dr. Wolfgang Gaertner

Phased-Array Antennas
by Dr. Arthur A. Oliner and George H. Knittel

Gallium Arsenide Microwave Bulk and Transit-
Time Devices
by Lester F. Eastman

Infrared-to-Millimeter Wavelength Detectors
by Frank R. Arams

Avalanche Transit-Time Devices
by George I. Haddad

Radar Detection and Tracking Systems
by S.A. Hovanessian

Microwave Filters for Communications Systems
by C.M. Kudsia and M.V. O'Donovan

Bubble Domain Memory Devices
by Alan Smith

Significant Phased Array Papers
by Dr. R.C. Hansen

Stripline Circuit Design
by Harlan Howe

Spectrum Analyzer Theory
and Applications
by Morris Engelson and Fred Telewski

ARTECH HOUSE, INC.
affiliated with Horizon House — Microwave, Inc.
610 Washington Street
Dedham, Massachusetts, 02026

ELECTRONIC INFORMATION PROCESSING

Physical Principles and Materials Technology

William V. Smith

ARTECH HOUSE

PHYS

Preface

Ever since its inception in the 1950's the electronic information processing industry has been experiencing the pangs of rebirth every half
dozen years or so. First generation vacuum tube computers were replaced by second generation transistorized computers, and in turn by
third generation computers using integrated circuits on semiconductor
chips for both logic and high speed memory. With each new generation the speed of individual computational steps and the amount of
rapidly accessible stored data have increased and the cost of manipulat-
ing and storing individual data bits decreased dramatically, resulting in
overall performance/price ratio improvements of orders of magnitude
There has been a symbiotic relationship between advances in electronic
solid state technology making possible these improvements in data
processing systems performance and the increased applications markets
made possible by improved systems performance forcing the technological advances. Where are these trends taking us? What is the shape of
the future in electronic information processing?

This book looks at possible technological futures through the eyes
of an industrial solid state physicist. We have already marched so far
down the road of miniaturization and integration that we find ourselves largely constrained to making use of the surface layers of solid
state electronic materials — layers of the order of one micrometer
thick. In this book we explore what different technologies, subject to
this constraint, have to offer in the way of further increases in speed,
miniaturization and integration of information processing circuits. The
technologies we explore are semiconductor, magnetic, optical and
superconducting ones.

These different technologies are, on the one hand, competitive with
each other for similar applications and, on the other hand, supplementary to each other for different applications. For example, semiconductor technology is firmly entrenched in high speed logic circuits, and
magnetic technology in large data base storage files, but semiconductors

v

have been displacing magnetic devices in high speed memory devices.
Will moving magnetic domains in fixed magnetic media (magnetic bubbles) invade the applications areas of moving magnetic media (disks and
tapes)? Optical technology is entrenched in input-output conversion
devices that interact with the human eye (either displaying an output
image or reading a written document). This book is not concerned
with these important applications but is concerned with to what extent optical technology can extend its base into the storage and high
speed data processing areas that are now the province of magnetic and
semiconductor technology. Finally, superconducting technology has
no current data processing stronghold. Can it establish a beachhead in
this field?

No final answers are given to these questions. However, trends and comparative analyses are developed in this one single reference book, using
a common mathematical and engineering language, and with the view-
point of one individual who has conducted or directed research (not
development) bearing on each of the areas analyzed.

Specifically, this book is the outgrowth of a series of tutorial talks prepared by the author during a two year period (1970–72) when he
directed the research of a small group of physicists at IBM's research
laboratory in Zurich, Switzerland. These talks in turn reflected his
prior experience directing a large group of physical scientists at IBM's
Thomas J. Watson Research Center in New York.

I am indebted to many colleagues for perceptive comment and con-
structive criticism, in particular to K.E. Drangeid for reviewing
Chapter 2 and W. Anacker and P.E. Seiden for reviewing Chapter 5.
I also wish to thank Frau Dilys Brulmann and her able staff in Zurich
for preparation of the original manuscript, and Mrs. Joyce Otis, Mrs.
Eileen Kavanaugh, and Miss Sue Lada for typing successive and
final versions of the text.

I dedicate the book to my mother, Mrs. Charles G. Smith, who has en-
couraged and inspired two generations of scientists.

Contents

Preface v

Chapter 1. Data Storage — on Surfaces or in Volume? 1
    High Density Data Storage and Minimum Bit Size ... 2
    Data Access, Access Time and Power Consumption .. 3
    Data Plane Organization 4
    Volume Organization of Data 9
    Organization of the Series 10
    References 11
    Problems 12

Chapter 2. Semiconductors 15
    Field-Effect Transistors 16
    Semiconductor Physics: Majority Carrier vs.
    Minority Carrier Devices 25
    Charge-Coupled Devices 28
    The Gunn Effect (Transferred Electron Devices) 31
    Other Semiconductor Devices: Two-Terminal vs.
    Three-Terminal Devices; Materials 35
    Bistable Memory Devices: Amorphous Semiconductors 36
    Summary 38
    References 39
    Problems 41

Chapter 3. Magnetic Information Storage 43
    Magnetic Bubble Devices 43
    Earlier Forms of Magnetic Storage 51
    Magneto-Optic Beam-Addressed Storage 56
    Magnetic Materials and the Physics of Magnetism 62
    Electrical Properties of Magnetic Materials 64

Contents

Summary 65
References 66
Problems 67

Chapter 4. Optics 69
Parallel Processing of Data or Materials 69
Coherence Properties of Lasers 72
Electro-Optic Phenomena 73
Planar Integrated Optics 80
Parallel Information Transmission by Coherent Light   81
Holographic Image Storage and Retrieval 82
Serial — Parallel Data Conversion 90
Serial Optical Processing, Data Transmission, and
Miniaturization 91
Input — Output; Display 94
Summary 95
References 95
Problems 97

Chapter 5. Superconductivity 101
Cryotron Memory and Logic Concepts 102
Physical Basis of Superconductivity 103
Flux Quantization and Energy Storage 106
The dc Josephson Effect 108
Magnetic Diffraction and Interference Phenomena;
Josephson Penetration Depth 110
The ac Josephson Effect 113
Devices 114
References 116
Problems 118

Epilogue 121

Answers to Problems 123

Figures

1-1.   Volume Data Storage   5-6
1-2.   Random Access to Data in a Plane   7-8
1-3.   Shift Register Access to Data in a Plane   9
2-1.   Schottky-Barrier Field-Effect Transistor   17
2-2.   Drift Velocity — Electric Field Curve   18
2-3.   FET I-V Characteristics   20
2-4.   Data Storage Circuits   22
2-5.   Use of Computer   23
2-6.   Performance Growth of Memories   24
2-7.   C-MOS Watch Circuit   25
2-8.   Planar Bipolar Transistor   27
2-9.   Charge-Coupled Device   29
2-10.   Simplified I-V and v-E Characteristics for GaAs   32
2-11.   Simplified Energy Band Picture for GaAs   33
2-12.   Simplfied Bistable Resistance Switching Characteristics   37
3-1.   Magnetic Bubbles   44
3-2.   T and I Bar Bubble Device   48
3-3.   Magnetic Bubble Materials   50
3-4A. 6μm Wide Bubble Tracks   52
3-4B.   A 100 Bit Shift Register   53
3-5.   Square Hysteresis Loop   54
3-6.   Thin-Film Memory Element   55
3-7.   Temperature Dependence of H_c and Mg   57
3-8.   Faraday Rotation   60
4-1.   Fourier Transformation and Filtering Operations   71
4-2.   Electro-Optic Modulation   75
4-3.   Acoustic-Optic Deflector   78
4-4A.   Wedge Technique for Producing a Two-Beam Hologram   83
4-4B.   The Reconstruction Process   83
4-5.   Holographic Memory System   84

4-6.   Magnetic Curie-point Hologram Written on a MnBi Thin
        Film 85-86
4-7.   Three Dimensional Holographic Recording 88-89
4-8.   Laser Inverter Circuit 92
5-1.   Cryotron Circuit 102
5-2A.   Electron Density of States in a Superconductor 105
5-2B.   Superconductive Tunneling Possibilities Across a Junction 105
5-3.   Quantized Flux Storage 107
5-4.   Josephson Tunneling 109
5-5.   Magnetic Diffraction Pattern for Josephson Tunneling 111-112
5-6.   Scanning Electron Micrograph of an Array of Josephson
        Junctions 115

Data Storage — on Surfaces or in Volume?

This book emphasizes electronic advances made possible by exploiting novel physical principles or by improved control over materials technology. In this introductory chapter however, we make the point that setting certain applications goals already tends to structure the technological implementation in simple physical ways. As an example, we will set ourselves the technological goal of trying to satisfy the data-storage requirements of a modern electronic computer. We soon realize that this is an open-ended problem. A computer is insatiable. It will find uses for the biggest, fastest storage system anyone can devise in the foreseeable future. A single high-quality aerial photograph contains roughly 10^{10} units of information storage, or bits, a factor of 10 larger than the online storage capacity of most large modern computers. The relatively straightforward task of electronically processing a single image may require 1,000 operations per bit, i.e., 10^{13} operations per image[1]. The vastly more complicated task of global weather forecasting could use 10^{19} bits[1]. And of course one wishes to perform these operations as rapidly as possible to get answers within a useful time-span.

Thus our applications goal is simple: the largest, fastest, cheapest, most reliable memory system possible.

We now seek to structure competitive systems within the physical constraints of the possible mechanisms available and also within what are thought to be the systems constraints. Examples of the latter are the optimum sizes of blocks of data and the generally desired reversibility of the data storage. Both types of constraints, of course, change with time and experience, and pushing the frontiers of physical limits often changes previously accepted philosophies of system constraints. Nonetheless, we shall see that there is a strong tendency for the presently accepted constraints to favor organizing a storage unit in stacks of two-dimensional, i.e., planar arrays. Such an organization, in turn, stresses the importance of surface phenomena. Strangely enough, we

1

shall also find that there is an alternative approach of dispersing the
data almost uniformly throughout a volume which cannot be lightly
dismissed, though it seems to present formidable difficulties.

1.1 HIGH-DENSITY DATA STORAGE AND MINIMUM BIT SIZE

There is an intimate relationship between the optimum configuration
of a data storage system and the physical phenomenon under consideration by means of which the data are stored.

Starting points in developing an ultimately self-consistent system
might be: what is the present optimum unit of data storage, and what
is its present optimum configuration? For example, in Chapter 3 we
analyze a data-storage unit of N atomic complexes, each carrying a
magnetic moment and in Chapter 4 we compare this approach with
a unit of N′ photochromic complexes (atomic complexes that change
color upon irradiation with light). These cases have quite different
optimum configurations. The N′ photochromic complexes are stable
as individual units. Often these units must be spread somewhat dilutely
throughout a matrix, to avoid mutual interactions which will degrade
the storage, although some recent materials can be used at high concentration[2]. On the other hand, the N magnetic complexes have useful storage properties only when strongly coupled in a ferromagnetic
or ferrimagnetic unit. If they are dispersed dilutely throughout a non-
magnetic matrix, they cannot be put into a stable ordered magnetic
state.

One consequence of the above considerations is that the theoretical
minimum unit of stored energy for a photochromic material is of the
order of an ultraviolet quantum of energy, 10^{-6} picojoules, which
can be localized in principle to perhaps 0.01 μm. In practice, the
resolution is determined by the resolution of the reading and writing
processes, both of the order of magnitude of an optical wavelength,
and the minimum practical unit of writing energy is more like 0.1 J
cm^{-2} or 10^3 picojoules per square micron spot.[3]

The calculations for a magnetic material are more involved and are related to less well-understood material properties (exchange energy,
saturation magnetization, anistropy, shape of specimen). In Chapter
3 we specifically analyze the case of thin magnetic films with regions
of reverse magnetization (magnetic bubbles) normal to the plane of
the film. Attainable material parameters include bubbles smaller than
1 μm in diameter in films of about the same thickness with a stored
magnetic energy of less than 10^{-3} picojoules. There are other ways of
storing energy — for instance in the phase changes of amorphous semiconductors (Chapter 2), in ferroelectric ceramics (Chapter 4), or in
superconducting circuits (Chapter 5), most of which can store data in

volumes of the order of one cubic micrometer but otherwise have widely differing characteristics. If we could position these data-storage units on a cubic lattice with 4.6 μm lattice spacing to isolate the units, we could store in one cubic centimeter of material the 10^{10} bits of information of our aerial-photograph example. In fact, such high storage densities are not presently in use and although some of the technologies mentioned permit speculation about their ultimate achievability, other considerations besides the density of storage enter into possible implementations.

1.2   DATA ACCESS, ACCESS TIME AND POWER CONSUMPTION

Let us assume that we do indeed have 10^{10} bits of information stored within a cube one centimeter on edge. Let us further assume that these bits are stored on a uniform lattice as discussed above, although we will also find that there are alternative storage possibilities, particularly in the photochromic example. What are some possible ways of accessing this data? How can we record it, how can we read it, and how can we alter it?

Consider the consequences of trying to address one bit at a time. It is difficult to achieve physical responses in any measuring equipment much faster than 100 picoseconds. Hence it would require at least one second to access the totality of data points in our memory. If we are seeking only a few specific data points, this would not be an efficient way to use the memory. However, we will wish to be accessing specific regions of memory at the maximum rate of data flow consistent with acceptable cost and power consumption at the attainable time constant τ. Hence, at this point, we can define a figure of merit which we will find useful in subsequent comparisons of specific electronic technologies. This is

$$E = P\tau, \tag{1-1}$$

the switching energy per bit already introduced in our examples of photochromic materials ($E_{PC} \cong 10^3$ picojoules) and magnetic bubble materials ($E_B \cong 10^{-3}$ picojoules). In Eq. (1-1), P represents the power consumption of the memory at the maximum sequential bit data flow rate

$$F = \tau^{-1}, \tag{1-2}$$

or 10^8 bits/sec in our example where τ = 100 picoseconds.

Note that the combination E = 1pJ, (intermediate between our photochromic and magnetic examples, τ = 100 ps, F = 10^8 bs^{-1}, implies P = 10 mw, a modest value of power consumption for an entire memory, but a somewhat high value for repeated access to the same bit location because of the difficulty of local dissipation of the power. Fortunately, the "word" or "page" organization of memories discussed below avoids this problem. Note also that $\tau = 100$ picoseconds is not physically attainable in all technologies — not, for example, in magnetic bubble technology — whereas it is attainable in the reading step of semiconductor technology ($E_{SC} \cong 1pJ$) and superconducting Josephson junction technology ($E_J \cong 10^{-6}$ pJ). Since nine orders of magnitude variation in E exist among materials considered for different applications, obviously other considerations besides this figure of merit enter into overall systems considerations. These include the distinctive features of optical access to information, which may outweigh the unfavorable value of E_{PC}, and the inconvenience of low temperature operation, which may outweigh the favorable value of E_J. Semiconductor memories have their disadvantages too: either their storage is transient, requiring frequent refreshing, or the writing and erasing process is relatively slow.

As already noted, information is always organized in a computer in minimum units of a "word" which may be, for example, 64 bits long. One could conceive of organizing the information in our cube on a superlattice of four lattice sites on an edge, each containing 4^3, or 64 bits of information (Fig. 1-1). Even a one-word-at-a-time access, however, would require a 16 millisecond cycle time through the entire memory — still rather slow. Thus the concept of sequential access throughout all the words stored in the memory is seen to be an undesirable way of locating the desired data.

What are the most "natural" physical subdivisions of the cube with its $N = 10^{10}$ information bits? They are either its $n = N^{1/3} = 2,150$ planes through lattice sites parallel to a cube plane, or its $m = N^{2/3} = 4,600,000$ lines through the sites parallel to an edge. These units contain respectively, 72,000 and 34 words which could be sequentially addressed in, respectively, 7.2 microseconds or 3.4 nanoseconds at the assumed achievable inquiry response time of 100 picoseconds. To implement such a partitioning requires a multiplicity of addressing and detecting equipment.

1.3 DATA PLANE ORGANIZATION

We see now that one useful way to look at our data-storage problems is to divide our 10^{10} bits, not uniformly throughout a volume, but rather into n planes of $10^{10}/n$ bits each (Fig. 1-1B). This also simplifies our data-access problem. We can separate the planes by some convenient distance and access them either over the surface or at the edges of the plane. Moreover, we have already noted that all the physical processes involved in our reading and writing the data generate un-

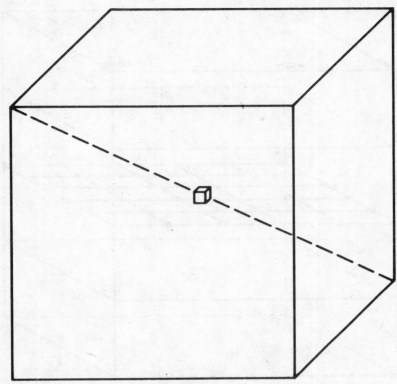

Figure 1-1. Volume Data Storage
                (A) Unstructured — How do we access this small cube?

desirable heat. This heat can be dissipated most conveniently in a
layered structure by convective cooling of the layers.

In our example we chose n = 2,150. We shall continue to use this
number, remembering however that we have more flexibility in
changing it now that we can use different criteria to optimize plane
size and plane spacing. For example, in a conventional magnetic recording disk pack, n ≈ 10.

We have divided the problem of data access into two steps: (1) pick
a plane and (2) find the data in the plane. Generally the data is well-
enough organized so that one knows in advance that the information
being sought is within one particular plane; hence, a system configuration that allows relatively slow access to a particular plane, but
rapid access within a plane, or even within several planes in parallel,
are also welcome. We may think of several data-processing configurations.

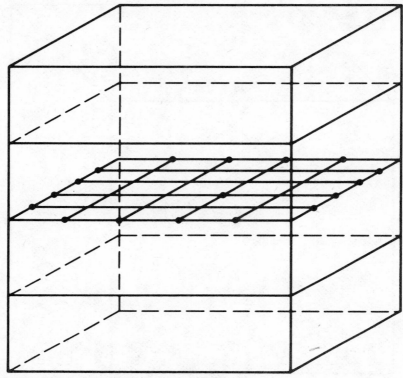

Figure 1-1. Volume Data Storage (cont.)
(B) Dataplane organization

a.   Integrated On-Plane Access

Accessing and sensing apparatus may be incorporated on each plane.
A pack of rotating magnetic disks with a separate reading head for
each plane is an example requiring mechanical motion. We consider
this to be already a conventional technology, and not a subject for
this book, but it is a technology which still has not been pushed to
its limit. Since it uses a continuous sheet of finely divided magnetic
material as the recording medium, it has a great advantage in cost
and simplicity over approaches based on single crystals despite the
handicap of mechanical motion. A major present technological chal-
lenge is to devise competitive, faster electronic systems that eliminate
the mechanical motion. For large n — perhaps 100 or 1000 — the requirement of multiplication of detection equipment is economically
feasible only if the detection equipment is inexpensive.

Integrated on-plane detection requires access to the data from the
edges of the plane. Figure 1-2 shows one option in handling the data:

Address reading or writing signals to the desired data point and collect the signal from that point. Present random-access memory organization uses this option. The writing and reading signals move along
electrical transmission lines connecting rows or columns of discrete
bits. The information bit is written at the intersection of two signal
lines, each of which enters and leaves the plane at two of its accessible
edges. Thus, the m bits in a plane can be addressed by only

$$\ell = 2\sqrt{m} \tag{1-3}$$

bit lines. In our example, access to 4,600,000 bits is achieved by
only 4,300 lines. The speed advantage of electrical access must be
balanced against the cost and complexity disadvantage of wiring the
individual bits. However, in Chapter 2, we shall note the present
efforts to adapt continuous recording media to this organization.

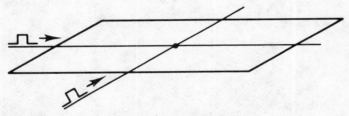

Figure 1-2.   Random Access to Data in a Plane
            (A) Interrogation pulses move to data at intersection of
                orthogonal signal lines

Fig. 1-2B illustrates two stages in the evolution of random access memories[4]. In the background of the photograph is a planar array of doughnut shaped, magnetic cores addressed by orthogonal wires threading
the holes of the doughnut. The information density is one bit per
core. In the center of the picture is an integrated semiconductor chip
measuring 0.284 cm on each side. The chip contains 64 bits of memory and has 664 components, representing a density of over 8,000
components per square centimeter. While this is still a far cry from
our hypothecated 4,600,000 bits per cm^2, progress continues apace
toward that goal and presently achieved bit densities are considerably
higher than those illustrated above.

In the second option, the data stream is moved to reading and writing stations on the edge of the plane (Fig. 1-3). Shift register approaches,
including charge transfer devices (Chapter 2) and magnetic bubbles
(Chapter 3) use this option. The recording medium is continuous,
which is an advantage, and although most embodiments still require

Figure 1-2.   Random Access to Data in a Plane (cont.)
(B) Monolithic bipolar integrated circuit technology is
used for buffer memory storage applications in IBM
System/360 Model 85, Model 195, and in the System/
370 Models 155 and 165. For such applications,
memory storage circuits are diffused into the surface
of a single silicon chip (shown above against a core
background) measuring less than an eighth-of-an-inch
square.   Each such chip — containing 664 individual
components such as transistors, diodes, and resistors —
provides 64 memory storage cells. These circuits
are so small that 53,000 components can fit into a
one square inch area.

relatively expensive single crystal materials, the recent discovery of a

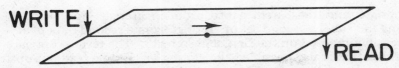

Figure 1-3.   Shift Register Access to Data in a Plane
The data moves between write and read stations, here
shown at the edges of the plane.

new class of amorphous magnetic bubbles materials[5] may revolution-
ize this technology. Access to any individual bit by this technique is
slower than in the random access mode since the entire data stream
must be moved from reading to writing station.

Incidentally, the disk pack uses a combination of data motion (the re-
volving disk) and address signal motion (the radial motion of the
reading head). Functionally, the mechanical transport of the data
under a fixed reading head over the rotating disk is equivalent to the
shift-register transfer of data through a fixed sheet to a fixed reading
head.

b. Separate Accessing Stations

One may design separate accessing equipment and move the selected
plane to the reading and writing stations. The advantage here is not
only a saving of equipment, but also the greater ease of direct access
over the face of the plane, perhaps by an optical or electron beam deflected to the desired data area. The surface is an inexpensive continuous sheet (Chapters 3 and 4). Also, if heat dissipation problems
are serious, they can be better solved in a separate, relatively spacious,
addressing station. The disadvantage is the slowness of the mechanical
step and the inability to address several planes in parallel. A hybrid
optical technique, however, enables one to move planar data subsets
in one large data plane to a single fixed data plane location
(Chapter 4).

The beam-addressable feature of separate accessing stations allows
their use in either a scanning or a random-access mode. The scanning
mode is functionally equivalent to the rotating disk or the shift-
register with a fixed reading head.

1.4 VOLUME ORGANIZATION OF DATA

In Chapter 4 we describe in some detail the interesting ability of optical techniques to transform an array of discrete data points in a plane
into a set of three-dimensional diffraction gratings superimposed on
each other in one volume of space — for example, a cube of some

appropriate semi-transparent photochromic material. Moreover, by
rotating the cube, a second set of gratings from a second data plane
can be superimposed on the first, and so forth. The reverse optical
transformation is also possible: the grating sets can be read out optically into planar data sets. The process is known as three-dimensional
holographic data storage.

For the purpose of this introductory chapter, it is sufficient for us to
know the following three points.

1.   There is a one to one correspondence between a particular point
     in a plane and a particular diffraction grating in the volume.

2.   In principle, the potential density of data storage in a cube of
     superimposed gratings, written and read optically by light of wave-
     length λ, is given by the optical resolution limit.

$$N = V/\lambda^3 \tag{1-4}$$

     For $V = 1$ cm^3 and $\lambda = 1$ μm, this limit is $N = 10^{12}$, i.e., our tar-
get of $N = 10^{10}$ seems to be a reasonable objective with this technology.

3.   At the present time, there is no known way to selectively erase
     small portions of old data (say the equivalent of one data plane)
     and record new data.

These points are sufficient to alert us to some of the attractive features
and problems of this technology. For instance, in common with
other forms of holographic memories (that store diffraction gratings
in planar sheets rather than volumes), the stored data is not easily degraded by scratches in the hologram. Whole data planes, or "pages"
are read simultaneously; i.e., the data is read in parallel, at the speed
of light. However, the non-erasability of the data is a serious draw-
back, and there are other practical points which we will address in
Chapter 4.

1.5 ORGANIZATION OF THE SERIES

In Chapter 2, we show how semiconductor technology is evolving,
partly in response to the system needs of compact, inexpensive,
rapidly accessed data, leading to arrays of integrated circuits on surfaces. Historically, of course, semiconductor technology arose in
response to the needs of analog circuits in the communications in-
dustries. The resulting discrete devices were easily adapted to high-
speed logic circuits. Although fewer logic than memory elements
are required, their interconnections are more complicated, leading

again to the requirement of arrays of integrated circuits on surfaces. We also discuss the discovery of the Gunn effect and its impact on microwave technology.

Chapter 3 shows how magnetic storage technology, which originally developed from the separate starting points of discrete circuits (cores) and continuous sheets (disks, tapes) is filling in the technological gap with semicontinuous structures (magnetic bubbles) and beam addressable memories. In order to treat the latter subject, we give a preliminary discussion of the optical properties of magnetic materials.

Chapter 4 treats optical technology more generally. Here the revolutionary advances of lasers and holography require a wide-ranging discussion of optoelectronics venturing beyond data processing to such diverse applications as radar and materials processing. We also expand on the comparisons of volume and surface data storage briefly touched upon in this introduction, and on the somewhat related subject of sequential vs. parallel data processing.

Chapter 5 takes a brief excursion into two topics of superconductivity, Josephson tunneling and quantized flux storage. The interest here is that some intrinsic physical limitations of these phenomena are indeed less restrictive than for competitive technologies. Speeds can be as fast as or faster than other electronic phenomena, and the accompanying energy dissipation much less. Difficult technolgical and economic problems remain, including systems acceptance of the potential storage volatility associated with low-temperature operation. (The volatility is less, however, than for semiconductor memories.) In some ways, this is an excellent example of planned industrial research, although the key element which was needed to give the whole concept any prospect of success — Josephson tunneling — was not planned. It is still an open question whether superconducting technolgy will prove competitive with present established technologies for data processing applications although it is, of course, well established in laboratory electronic and some industrial "heavy-equipment" applications such as permanent magnets.

REFERENCES

1.　W.H. Ware, "The Ultimate Computer," IEEE Spectrum *9*. No. 3, 84–91, (1972).

2.　W.J. Tomlinson, E.A. Chandross, R.L. Fork, C.A. Pryde and A.A. Lamola, "Reversible Photodimerization: A New Type of Photochromism," Applied Optics *11*, 533–548 (1972).

3.   O.N. Tufte and D. Chen, "Optical Techniques for Data Storage", IEEE Spectrum 10, 26–32, (Feb. 1973).

4.   R.W. Landauer, "The Future Evolution of The Computer," Physics Today *23*, 22–28 (July 1970).

5.   P. Chaudhari, J.J. Cuomo and R.J. Gambino, "Amorphous Metallic Films for Bubble Domain Applications," IBM J. Res. Develop. *17*, 66–68, (1973).

PROBLEMS

1.1 The power dissipation requirements of logic circuits are more severe than those of memory circuits because the former are frequently run at high duty cycles. Consider a thin flat silicon chip whose surface is densely populated with logic circuits. Assume the active area of each circuit to be $100 \mu m^2$, the thickness of the silicon chip $400 \mu m$ and its thermal conductivity $1.2 W/cm°C$. For a 10% duty cycle in each circuit, what would be the temperature rise in the center of the chip for logic circuits dissipating, respectively, 10^3, 1 and 10^{-3} picojoules per 100 picosecond switching event?

1.2 In problem 1.1, what is the total power dissipation in a 0.1 cm² area chip assuming 10% coverage of active circuits in the three cases? How many circuits are involved?

1.3 What is the longest possible path delay interconnecting logic circuits on a chip with active circuits confined to a 0.3 cm by 0.3 cm area? Assume only horizontal and vertical connecting paths (i.e., parallel to the chip edges) and a single propagation velocity two thirds that of light in vacuum.

1.4 In magnetic bubble technology (Chapter 3) shift registers are currently operable at a 100 kHz cycle rate.

a.   What is the maximum access time to a one dimensional 1,000 bit shift register with a single detecting station using this technology? The average access time?

b.   If the register can shift in two dimensions, what is the maximum access time to a 10^6 bit (1,000 x 1,000) shift register with a single detecting station?

c.   If the cycle rate can be improved to one megacycle, what would the access time be to a two dimensional 10^8 bit shift register?

d.   If the memory in c is partitioned into 10^4 square pages each containing 10^4 bits with one detector per page, what is the cycle time?

e. Assuming a memory cell spacing of 10μm, what is the physical size of the above 10^8 bit memory?

1.5 In a beam addressed memory the temperatures determining the process differ markedly from those in a logic plane (problem 1). The transient temperature rise of a rapidly — and infrequently — addressed bit is primarily determined by its heat capacity rather than by heat conduction. Assuming a volume heat capacity C of 0.5 calories /cm^3 and no conduction losses, what is the transient temperature rise of a 1μm^3 bit that absorbs, respectively, 10^3, 1 and 10^{-3} picojoules of energy? (1 calorie $4\approx$ joules; $\dfrac{Q}{V}$ = C Δ T).

Semiconductors

The importance of surfaces in modern electronic technology was made plausible in Chapter 1. In the present chapter, we develop specific device and materials analyses for typical high-speed logic and small, fast, memory circuits which in today's computers are based on semiconductor conduction processes. Indeed, we are able to specialize further to silicon as the semiconductor, and to fabrication and interconnection of devices on silicon surfaces.

This degree of materials specialization is one sign of technological maturity. The ability to tailor different materials to specific applications, as is the case for photoelectric surfaces, photoluminescent phosphors, and magnetic materials, can also be a sign of maturity. However, with semiconductors one material can be tailored to a number of applications. Among other things, this fact simplifies a discussion of the fundamental physical principles involved, and is one reason for selecting semiconductors as our first technology. We defer a discussion of optical interactions in semiconductors, which do require consideration of a wider variety of materials, to Chapter 4.

Not all semiconductor devices require single crystals, although the time constants of amorphous or polycrystalline devices are slower than those those of optimized single crystal devices. Nonetheless, the material and processing costs of amorphous materials are so much less than those of optimized single crystals that the former may be preferable where the cost side of cost-performance tradeoffs is emphazised. Most of this chapter stresses the performance side of the tradeoff, for which single-crystal silicon has achieved universal industrial acceptance.

We describe three types of integrated semiconductor devices: bipolar transistors, field-effect transistors, and charge-coupled devices, which show an increasing trend to utilization of thin surface layers of nearly homogeneous semiconductors. Field-effect transistors are discussed first, since they are conceptually the simplest and most susceptible to an elementary analysis, which we develop in Section 2-1.

The fact that highly-doped uniform surface layers are the important active ingredients of integrated semiconductor devices lends encouragement to the speculation that further evolution may yet remove the requirement of single crystals for wider classes of applications than is presently the situation. Hence the unique role of silicon may yet diminish in the future. The chapter ends with a discussion of bistable semiconductor conductivity states exhibited by a variey of materials, both single crystal and amorphous, which illustrate this possibility. In contrast to the earlier examples, the physics involved here is far from being well understood.

The Gunn oscillator, which we also discuss to some extent, probably would have evolved ultimately as the fruition of a planned research program on extending the high frequency range of microwave oscillators. In fact, however, it actually emerged as an unanticipated by-product of a basic research program on noise in semiconductors. Hence necessity, here, was not the mother of invention, but one looks to see whether invention can create new necessities (or better satisfy old ones).

2.1 FIELD-EFFECT TRANSISTORS

Semiconductors can exhibit many complicated conduction phenomena. However, some of the most useful devices at present are also the simplest. These field effect transistors (FET) are based on control of the current by controlling the density N and the velocity v of majority charge carriers (i.e., carriers of one sign only). Denoting the magnitude of the charge by e, this current density is

$$j = N e v \qquad\qquad\qquad (2\text{-}1)$$

Current flows from source S through a channel controlled by a gate G to a drain D (see Fig. 2-1). The maximum velocity of the electrons is determined by the source-drain voltage, V_D, and their number primarily by the gate voltage V_G which determines the width of the entrance to the channel.

As is evident from the figure, the actual geometry is three-dimensional, with considerable nonuniformity in the current flow. Nonetheless, some of the properties of the device can be understood by simplifications based on a homogeneous channel.

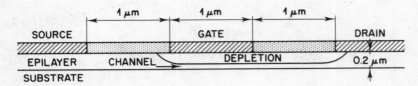

F E T

Figure 2-1. Schottky-barrier field-effect transistor. Modulation of the gate voltage controls the width of the depletion layer, and hence the width of the channel in which current flows from source to drain. The insulating substrate and N-doped conducting epilayer are of single-crystal silicon, on which metal electrodes (shaded) are evaporated. The interelectrode spaces are protected by SiO_2 (dotted) grown from the silicon.

Consider Eq. (2-1) applied to a homogeneous volume, with an electric field E in the direction of the current flow. The velocity is a function of E, often the form shown in Fig. 2-2. In the initial linear portion

$$v = \mu E \qquad\qquad\qquad (2\text{-}2)$$

where μ is the mobility of the charge carriers. At high fields the velocity saturates to a value v_s.

For magnitudes we take the following values as typical of a silicon FET at room temperature:[1]

$$\mu \; = 500 \; cm^2/V \; sec.$$

$$v_s \; = 10^7 \; cm/sec. \qquad\qquad\qquad (2\text{-}3)$$

$$N \; = 5 \times 10^{16}/cm^3.$$

For a typical response time we take the transit time over a 1 μm distance (a typical gate length, ℓ) at the limiting velocity

$$\tau = \frac{\ell}{v_s} = 10^{-4}/10^7 = 10 \text{ picoseconds} \qquad\qquad (2\text{-}4)$$

We calculate the power dissipation per unit volume as

$$P_V = j_s E_s = N e \; v_s E_s = N e \; v_s^2/\mu \qquad\qquad (2\text{-}5)$$

where we have approximated the saturation characteristic of the semiconductor by joining a constant low-field mobility section with the

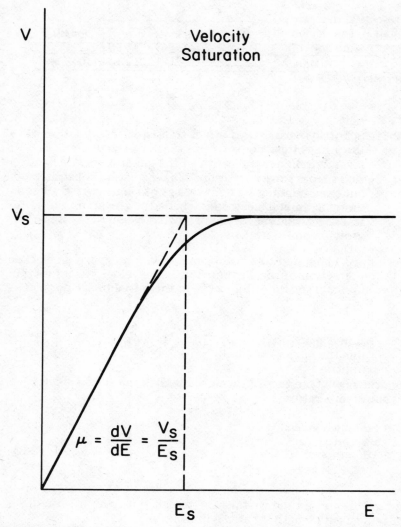

Figure 2-2. Drift velocity — electric field curve. In silicon electrons drift at a constant mobility μ at low fields and a constant velocity v_s at high fields exceeding a critical field E_s.

saturated velocity at $v_s = \mu E_s$. Equation (2-5), with the magnitudes of Eq. (2-3), gives

$$P_V = 1.6 \times 10^{-3} \text{ watts}/\mu m^3$$

An experimental device dimension is $\ell = 1 \mu$m, d, the slab thickness = 0.2 μm, and b, the device width = 100 μm,[1-3] giving V = 20 μm³ and a device power-time constant product (a figure of merit) of

$$P_\tau = 0.3 \text{ picojoules} \tag{2-6}$$

close to the value of 1 picojoule for E_{SC} quoted in Chapter 1. Note also that this device, operated at a 50% duty cycle must dissipate 16 milliwatts of power, a consideration helping determine the maximum packing density of logic devices.

The mobility and limiting velocity of Eqs. (2-3) are determined by the material, but the carrier density N is subject to design. In essence, the design criterion is that N be as large as possible subject to the restriction that the space charge developed does not become so high that the drain voltage no longer influences the current. If the mobility were constant, then in a slab of thickness d and permittivity $\epsilon \epsilon_0$, this would take place when the source-drain voltage v_D reached a value[1,4] (approximately)

$$V_{DS} = N e d^2 / 2 \epsilon \epsilon_0 \tag{2-7}$$

A two dimensional space charge limited conduction analysis shows that at this value the current becomes "pinched off" at the drain end of the gate and little further increase of current with drain voltage is possible. The result is a group of I – V characteristics like those of Fig. 2-3.

At low currents, where space charge can be neglected, a similar group of I – V characteristics occurs with a knee at the voltage

$$V'_{DS} = E_s \ell = v_s \ell / \mu \tag{2-8}$$

corresponding to the saturation of the drift velocity at the field E_s in Fig. 2-2, and conductivity according to Eq. (2-1) with N constant. V'_{DS} therefore is the maximum value of V_{DS} so that an optimum device design occurs when $V_{DS} \simeq V'_{DS}$, whence

$$\tau = \ell^2 / \mu V_{DS}' \text{ and} \tag{2-9}$$

$$P_\tau = \frac{2 \epsilon \epsilon_0 \ell B V_{DS}^2}{d} \tag{2-10}$$

$V'_{DS} = 2$ volt for the magnitudes of Eqs. (2-3) and (2-4). This gives for N the value

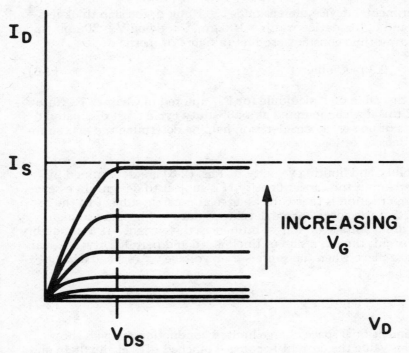

Figure 2-3. FET I-V characteristics. For constant mobility, the maximum FET drain current I_s saturates at a voltage V_{DS} determined by space charge considerations. Curve A may be identified as the O binary state and B as 1.

$$N = \frac{2\,\epsilon\,\epsilon_0 V_s \ell}{\mu\,e\,d^2} \tag{2-11}$$

Operating at or near the knee of the bends in Fig. 2-3 saturates the transconductance $\partial I/\partial V_g$ at its maximum value and maximizes the voltage gain. From Eq. (2-10), the ratio of dissipative switching energy, $P\tau$, to stored capacitive energy, $CV_D^2/2$, is four. (See Eq. (2-16) for a visualization of the high frequency amplifier properties of the device in terms of the more familiar gain bandwidth product.)

In Eq. (2-1), ℓ is fixed at the smalled practical value (about $1\,\mu$m) by the requirement of minimizing τ, Eq. (2-4). Maximizing N results from minimizing d. However, increasing N also results in decreasing another critical quantity, E_B, the breakdown field at which impact ionization occurs at the drain end of the gate. It is necessary to maintain E_B larger than E_s. These considerations set a lower limit of about 0.2 μm for d.[1] This is also a well-controllable dimension since it is determined by the technology of epitaxial growth rather than photolithography. The resulting numerical relation for P_v then, using the value $\epsilon \, \epsilon_0 = 10^{-12}$ coulomb volt cm appropriate to Si, is

$$N = 6 \times 10^{16}/cm^3$$

approximately the value given in Eqs. (2-3). If, by considering other materials, one also has control over μ and v_s, we see that Eq. (2-4) and the maximization of N by Eq. (2-11) require that

v_s be as large as possible   (2-12)

and

μ be as large as possible.

We recognize that in attaining these FET characteristics we are talking about the properties of surface layers a fraction of a micron thick. Actually, the surface properties are even more important than the brief analysis above indicates. Communication with, or isolation from, the outside world is achieved at the surface. Two important classes of metal-semiconductor surfaces are illustrated in Fig. 2-1. The source and drain contacts must be ohmic, and of low resistance, whereas the gate contact must be insulating. This is achieved either by a Schottky barrier — a region in the semiconductor depleted of charge carriers by the contact potential difference of metal to semiconductor — or by incorporating an added insulating layer, conveniently SiO_2, between the silicon and the metal. The importance and difficulty of control of surfaces is evident from the fact that the FET concept was proposed at least as early as the 1930's[5] (other sources quote still earlier proposals) well before the discovery of the bipolar transistor.[6] The concept was independently re-investigated in 1948[7] and 1952,[4] but it required an additional dozen years of materials research before this simple form of transistor began to achieve practicality.

The above catalog of FET properties has emphasized their speed, low power consumption and simplicity of fabrication. All those properties are obviously ideal for their use as logic circuits where no information storage is required, but how can they be used in memory as mentioned in Chapter 1? The answer is that the gate electrode (Fig. 2-1) also has the property of transient charge storage: It takes time for charge to leak off a floating gate through the very high resistance depletion layer. Hence, one can write a 0 or 1 into the transistor by pulsing the gate at $V_{GO} = A$ or $V_{G1} = B$ (leaving different charges stored on the gate) and can read the circuit by pulses on the

Figure 2-4. Data Storage Circuits: Silicon chips, each about one-eighth-inch square, contain 1024 microscopically small monolithic data storage units used in IBM System/370 Models 158 and 168 (Figure courtesy IBM).

drain resulting in low (preferably zero) or high output current pulses respectively. Such a mode of operation requires periodic refreshing of the gate voltages to compensate for the charge leakage, plus maintaining a continuous low drain voltage operating point to preserve a suitable depletion layer.

Fig. 2-4 shows a higher density storage unit than Fig. 1-2B — one where the individual circuit detail of the 1024 storage bits in each one eighth inch square chip is lost to the eye. Only the connections from the edge of the chips to the outside world are evident.

Finally, one should note an important further technological advance. Incorporating a more complicated gate insulation structure results in much longer storage times (months or years) even without standby power.[8] The essential step is to deposit a Si_3N_4 insulating layer on top of the SiO_2 layer. (The device is called a MNOS — standing for Metal Nitride Oxide Semiconductor-transistor, and there are further variations.) In this device the stored charge is driven into the $SiO_2 - Si_3N_4$ interface by a relatively high and long gate (write 1) pulse, altering the threshold gate voltage (V_{GO} = A, Fig. 2-3) semi-permanently. An appropriate negative erase (write 0) pulse will restore the original condition. The resulting structure for all of those devices resembles Fig. 1-2B, but, as in Fig. 2-4, the circuit detail is lost to the eye.

Reexamining Fig. 1-2B, and extrapolating the fabrication challenges to orders of magnitude more bits and smaller circuits makes it clear

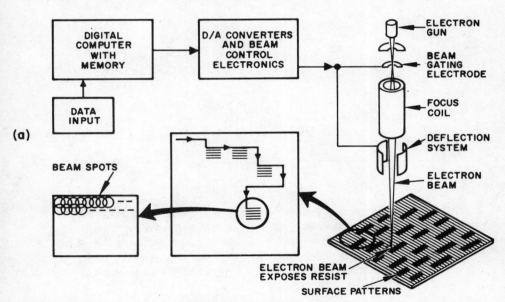

Figure 2-5.   Use of computer — controlled electron beam to draw patterns of electron sensitive resist.
(From reference 9, with permission of Solid State Technology.)

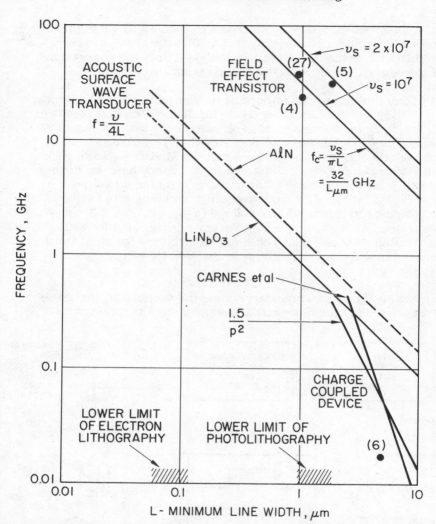

Figure 2-6. Performance growth of memories; area and power per bit are shown vs. time for several types of memories. The points beyond 1972 represent projections based on electron beam fabrication. (From reference 9, with permission of Solid State Technology and Hughes Research Laboratories.)

that new processing technologies are required to meet these challenges. Some of these are the use of electron and ion beams under program-med computer control in the fabrication steps.[9] The schematics of such control are shown in Fig. 2-5, and the resulting achieved and extrapolated bit dimensions and high frequency performance for a number of related devices in Fig. 2-6 (MOS≡FET; we discuss bipolar and CCD devices in the next two sections). Fig. 2-7 shows a modern electronic watch circuit made by this technology.

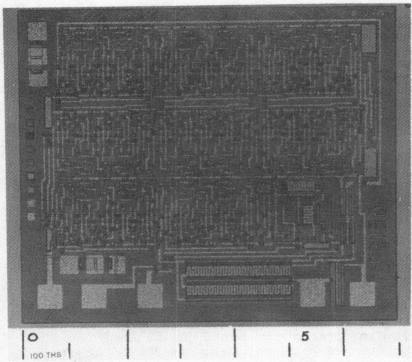

Figure 2-7. C-MOS watch circuit combines oscillator, 16 stage binary divider and output driver on one chip. (From reference 9, with permission of Solid State Technology.)

2.2 SEMICONDUCTOR PHYSICS; MAJORITY CARRIER VS MINORITY CARRIER DEVICES

A basic understanding of the two semiconductor properties singled out for discussion in the preceding section — mobility and limiting velocity of majority carriers — relies on the extensive background of semiconductor physics built up over the last two decades. There are many good texts on this subject, some including device analyses.[10] The energy band picture is the theoretical starting point, and with it the concept of an effective mass of the electrons. This together with a catalog of the various scattering mechanisms of the electrons —

both with the impurities required to achieve desired doping levels, (thus determining N), and with the host lattice — are ingredients of the theory. Moreover these scattering processes are energy dependent — hence the limiting velocity. All these are traditional research areas in bulk semiconductor physics, equally applicable to epitaxial thin film layers.

Other semiconductor physics concepts enter into the properties of other devices; properties of minority carriers, injection of minority carriers across surfaces and at p-n junctions, tunneling, avalanche break-down, transfer of carriers from high-mobility to low-mobility subbands, recombination of carriers, etc. Many of these either intrinsically involve surfaces or can be profoundly modified near surfaces and perhaps by other effects of geometrical inhomogeneity in the transport.

The original bipolar semiconductor transistors controlled the current of minority carriers injected across p-n or n-p junctions.[6]   A modern planar version of such a transistor with an n+ emitter and n+ buried collector is shown in Fig. 2-8.[11] Why are the majority carrier transport devices like the FET transistor of Fig. 2-1 preferred for some applications?

There are two reasons. First, the structure of Fig. 2-1 is clearly simpler so that it is likely to be more easily, cheaply, and reliably made, and to closer tolerances. These considerations favor applications requiring inexpensive integrated structures, and we shall subsequently see in charge-coupled devices[12] even simpler structures. The second advantage of majority carrier transport is that it is usually faster than for minority carriers. In the n p n transistor of Fig. 2-8, for example, a uniformly doped (N=constant) central p region is essentially free of electric field at low currents. Electrons injected from the emitter move by diffusion to the collector, where the concentration is much lower. At high currents the accompanying electric field enhances this diffusion and the time τ_D for them to traverse the distance ℓ to the buried collector is given by [13]

$$\tau_D = \ell^2/2D \qquad\qquad\qquad (2\text{-}13)$$

Here D, the coefficient of diffusion, is given by the Einstein relation

$$D = \frac{kT}{e}\,\mu \approx 0.026\,\mu \qquad\qquad\qquad (2\text{-}14)$$

For the magnitudes of Eqs. (2-3), with $\ell = 1\ \mu m$, τ_D is 400 picoseconds. In practice, RC time constants are a still more severe limitation in

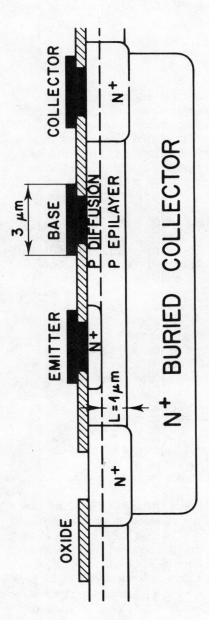

Figure 2-8. Planar bipolar transistor. Complicated processing steps result in a transistor whose electrodes are accessible at a planar surface, although the rate-limiting conduction steps occur in the vertical dimension. Minority carriers (electrons) are injected from the N+ emitter and travel through the P base to the N+ buried collector. Changes in the small fraction of these carriers that recombine with the majority carriers in the base region (I_B) control the larger current I_C.

these devices, by perhaps a factor of 10. Experimental values of P_{T_D} in devices of approximately the dimension of Fig. 2-8 are as low as 5 picojoules.[11]

2.3 CHARGE-COUPLED DEVICES

The most recent addition to the family of integrated semiconductor devices replaces microscopic tailoring of the semiconductor surface (Fig. 2-8) by a completely homogeneous semiconductor with all the required control elements consisting of insulated metal electrodes deposited on the surface (Fig. 2-9). Consider first the top figure (A). The semiconductor region (n type) under the group of electrodes that is charged to the voltage $-V_1$ (typically –5 volts) is in a stable state where the dashed line indicates the level of the depletion layer (no mobile charge carriers). Electrodes 1 and 7, charged to $-V_2$ (-10 volts) also have a stable semiconductor configuration. The high negative voltage stabilizes a thin surface layer with an excess of mobile positive charge, i.e., a p type inversion layer. The semiconductor region under electrodes 4 and 10, however — also charged to $-V_2$ — is in a metastable condition, supporting a depletion region without an inversion layer. This is possible because in well-prepared silicon it takes time for the p inversion layer to form. The required minority carriers must be generated thermally in the bulk (or at defect states at the surface which can be kept few in number by good processing) and then be attracted to the surface by the negative voltage. The equilibrium number is determined by the balancing forces of the electric field and the concentration gradient. Before the inversion layer forms, the material is in a metastable state, where only a depletion layer exists. Initial conditions determining the presence or absence of the inversion layer will be discussed shortly.

Consider now Fig. 2-9B. Here a still more negative voltage $-V_3$ (-15 volts) has been applied to electrodes 2, 5, 8 and 11. The mobile surface charge previously trapped under 1 and 7 now moves under 2 and 8 and, when in Fig. 2-9C, $-V_3 \rightarrow -V_1$ on 2, 5, 8 and 11 and $-V_2 \rightarrow -V_1$ on 1, 4, 7 and 10, stays trapped on these electrodes. Thus one can see that a properly-chosen time sequence of electrode voltages moves trapped charge along the semiconductor. In Fig. 2-9, the sequence of voltage changes is three phase and charge can be stored under every third electrode, isolated from one another by the potential hill on each side. The cyclic advance of the charge pattern to the right forms a shift-register with input at 1 and output at 11. Separate devices are necessary to control the input and detect the output. For example, the holes can be injected at the edge of the semiconductor slab by a conventional p-n junction. However, an entire charge pattern can

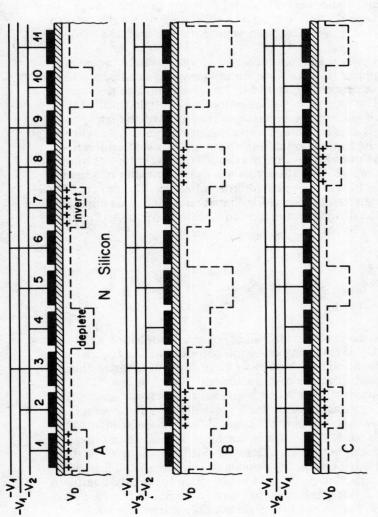

Figure 2-9. Charge-coupled device. Trapped charge can be moved along the surface of a homogeneous semiconductor by a properly-timed sequence of voltage pulses to a cyclic electrode structure.

also can be generated over the surface by an appropriate pattern of light, the light generating p-n pairs in the depletion layer, with the positively charged holes moving to the surface and the electrons to the lower boundary of the depletion layer under the influence of the electric field. Thus, this phenomenon is useful in image-sensing devices.[14] An image written over the surface of a CCD chip by a light pattern can be read out at an edge by successive shift register steps.

These devices have no gain and hence are more suitable for memory than for logic applications. They are in many ways analogous to (and the concept was probably inspired by) magnetic-bubble devices (Chapter 3). The magnetic configuration is essentially multistable, however, in contrast to the metastable character of the free charge analog. There is also at present some loss of charge in successive transfer steps, and the fundamental limitations are not well understood. For example, in present devices, maximum cycling rates are in the few megahert region. One theory of the charge transfer mechanism predicts a much higher speed capability, however. The concept involved is "field-driven diffusion-like" motion with a time constant for the charge to diffuse away from an electrode of length ℓ given by a relation similar to Eq. (2-9):[12,15]

$$\tau_{cc} = \frac{\ell^2}{\mu V} \tag{2-15}$$

$$GB = (2\Pi\tau_{cc})^{-1} \tag{2-16}$$

where V is the excess electrode voltage over threshold for a field-effect transistor and GB is the gain-bandwidth product of the transistor. Although the technology is still in an early stage of investigation, typical experimental values of ℓ are already 10 μm or less.[9,14] The mobility of holes in silicon is less than that of electrons, giving 200 cm^2/V sec as a reasonable value for μ (actually an effective mobility somewhat lower than the true bulk mobility). These numbers give 10 nanoseconds for τ_{cc}, about a factor of 100 faster than observed under conditions of very high efficiency (99.98%) charge transfer. However, Eq. (2-15) essentially applies to transfer of the initial 50% or so of the charge, and a 100-fold longer time for nearly complete charge transfer is not unreasonable. Extrapolating to ten-fold smaller electrodes (ℓ = 1 micron) suggests possible achievable time constants

$$\tau_{cc} = 10 \text{ to } 100 \text{ nanoseconds} \tag{2-16}$$

for charge-coupled devices, several hundred times slower than the Schottky barrier field-effect transistors. The figures of merit of the

two devices are quite comparable however. For charge transfer devices

$$P_{Tcc} = E_{cc} = \frac{CV^2}{2} \qquad\qquad (2\text{-}17)$$

which, for $\ell = 10\ \mu m$, $\epsilon\epsilon_0 = 10^{-12}$ and $V = 4$ volt has the value 0.8
picojoules. One can perhaps extrapolate to a ten times smaller figure.

If we compare charge-coupled devices with magnetic bubbles we
find that the electrode connections required for the former are a de-
cided disadvantage, perhaps more fundamental than the imperfect
charge transfer efficiency and limited storage times. The latter two
problems can perhaps be circumvented by improved technology for
the first point and suitable systems design (i.e., not requiring long
storage time) for the second.

2.4 THE GUNN EFFECT (TRANSFERRED ELECTRON DEVICES)

The new devices described to this point — the field-effect transistor
and charge-coupled devices — both represent the hoped-for results of
planned applied research. On the other hand, the Gunn oscillator[16]
was the "cultivated" by-product of a basic research program, in an
industrial laboratory (IBM) on the sources of noise in semiconductors.
Tracing down the origin of a particular type of fairly regular high frequency noise led J.B. Gunn to discover a new class of useful high-
frequency oscillators and amplifiers.

The particular technological thrust we have been emphasizing so far —
did not lead naturally to this investigation. On the other hand, a different but simultaneous trend — seeking to extend the high-frequency
range of oscillators — had already initiated research on novel principles for two terminal negative resistance semiconductor devices. In
fact, as a result of such research at a second industrial laboratory
(Mullard) the theoretical foundation for interpreting Gunn's oscillations had already been laid.[17] The connection between the two independent research paths was soon made.[18]

A simple description of the Gunn effect is as follows. When an
electric field is developed across electrodes at the parallel ends of
certain single-crystal semiconductors, GaAs being the original and,
to date, best example, high-frequency oscillations appear when the
field exceeds a characteristic value. Except for very short samples,
$\ell < 100\ \mu m$, the oscillation frequency is more characteristic of the
sample length than of the circuit, and is inversely proportional to the
sample length.

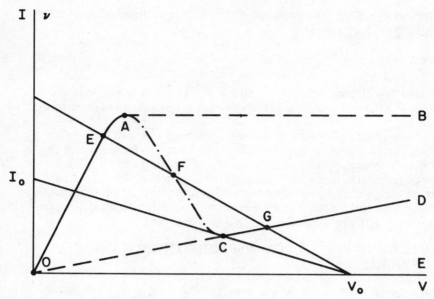

Figure 2-10. Simplified I-V and v-E characteristics for GaAs. The low field, high-conductivity region OA is connected to the high field, low-conductivity region CD by the negative resistance characteristic AC. Two load lines are drawn. In the upper one oscillation occurs about the unstable intersection F between the limits E and G.

The circuit aspects of this phenomenon can be understood by reference to Fig. 2-10 which shows schematically the electron velocity — electric field characteristic OACD of n-type GaAs, or equivalently (for a fixed carrier concentration and spatially uniform electric field), the I-V characteristic. It is to be contrasted with the saturated velocity curve OAB (also shown in Fig. 2-2) of silicon. The negative resistance region AFC can be viewed as a generator for the high-frequency oscillations. For a fixed voltage source V_o somewhat greater than that at the current minimum C, as the series resistance is decreased from infinity, the steady-state operating point moves along the line OEA. When the resistance is less than V_o/I_o three intersections with the load line appear, such as those at E, F, and G. If V_o is large enough, the stable solution is an oscillatory one, with current and voltage swings between E and G. As already noted, the physical explanation of this negative resistance was understood, and the resulting amplification and oscillation predicted several years before Gunn's observations.[17] As with the FET, the concept preceded adequate con-

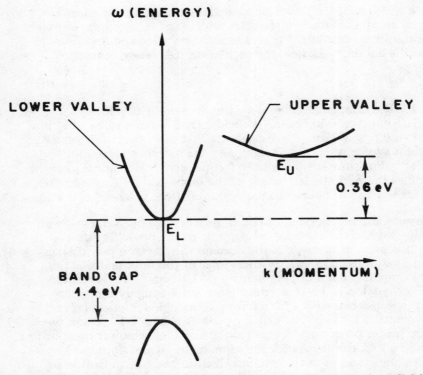

Figure 2-11. Simplified energy band picture for GaAs. At low fields all conduction electrons are in the high mobility lower valley minimum (region OE, Figure 2-10). At high fields a large portion of the electrons are transferred to the lower mobility upper valley (region GD).

trol over the materials and the first attempt at experimental verification was a failure.[19]

A brief description of the physics follows. At low electric fields the electrons in the conduction band of GaAs all lie near the lowest energy minimum E_ϱ (Fig. 2-11), which has a characteristic high mobility μ_ϱ. At high electric fields the electron temperature, i.e., the average electron energy, is raised 0.36 eV to the point where most of the electrons are transferred into the minimum of a higher-lying energy band E_u which happens to have a lower mobility μ_u. This accounts for the sections OE and GD of the I-V characteristic. The dynamics result from the fact that near the point E of the I-V characteristic a thin high field domain builds up near the cathode of the device and, at slightly higher voltages, breaks loose from the cathode and travels to the anode at a characteristic speed approximately that of the steady-state drift velocity at E. For long samples, a second domain breaks off from the cathode when the first domain reaches the anode.[16] Hence, the oscillation frequency is, roughly,

$$v = v_D/\ell \qquad\qquad (2\text{-}18)$$

where ℓ is the sample length and v_D the domain drift velocity. For $v_D \approx 10^7$ cm/sec, as in GaAs, (coincidently the same value of v_s in silicon), and $\ell = 100~\mu$m, $v = 1$ gigahertz. At this operating point E the field is typically 1650 volts/cm, and the mobility μ_ℓ 6,000 cm/volt.[20] For shorter samples the frequency of the resonant circuit determines the periodic launching of the domains.[21] (This is known as the LSA, Limited Space change Accumulation, mode of operation.)

The physics and engineering of Gunn devices have been pursued substantially beyond the sketchy description given above.[10] For example, it is known that within the domain the electron density can peak to a value perhaps twenty times that of the bulk material outside the domain. For a doping density of 10^{14} cm^{-3} the domain in GaAs is calculated to be an accumulation layer roughly one micrometer thick in series with a 20 micrometers thick depletion layer.[20] Since operation is to the right of the peak A in Fig. 2-10, Gunn devices are higher power devices (requiring also higher power dissipation) than field-effect transistors for the same material and doping. Moreover, the objectives of device miniaturization and maximization of the operating frequency can be shown to require an increase in N at least to the range of 10^{15} to 10^{16} cm^{-3}. Equation (2-5), replacing v_s by v_D and E_s by E_A, may be treated as a rough measure of the threshold power per unit volume, which is seen to be proportional to N. The device performance is ultimately limited by its heat-dissipation problems.

The structural and fabrication simplicity of two terminal negative-resistance devices such as the Gunn oscillator is a great advantage for discrete microwave oscillators and amplifiers (the use of circulators allows a two-terminal device to be used as an amplifier), and miniaturization is relatively straight-forward. Typically, the active region is an epitaxial layer of n GaAs, perhaps $10~\mu$m thick, grown on a high-conductivity n+ GaAs substrate. The wafer is diced into small chips and metal electrodes deposited on top and bottom for convenient connection to a microwave cavity or strip line.[22] This is seen to be an attractively simple structure for this application.

Two terminal devices do not lend themselves naturally to logic circuits. However, the launching of a Gunn domain is essentially a fast, digital event. Hence some research effort has been devoted to the goal of adding a control electrode to the Gunn diode.[22] This is best accomplished in a planar technology where all the electrodes are on the surface of a thin ($2\ \mu$m) epitaxial layer of GaAs on an insulating substrate. This geometry is also appropriate to traveling-wave Gunn amplifiers, eliminating the need for a circulator, and it has some potential advantages for heat dissipation.[22] As with injection lasers (Chapter 4) it is questionable whether Gunn logic devices will prove competitive with other semiconductor logic devices in transit time and $P\tau$ figures of merit. Recently quoted figures[23] are $\tau = 50$ to 100 ps and $P\tau = 1$ to 10 pJ.

As a final point one should add that there is a continuing search for materials superior to GaAs, and there are some promising results[24,25] but it is premature to conclude that they will become competitive with GaAs.

2.5 OTHER SEMICONDUCTOR DEVICES: TWO-TERMINAL VS. THREE-TERMINAL DEVICES; MATERIALS

We shall not discuss in detail other semiconductor single-crystal devices such as tunnel diodes, and avalanche transistors.[10] They are based on others of the phenomena mentioned in Section 2-2 and are subject to analogous analysis. Obviously, the relevant physical parameters of each process must be known and be describable by sufficiently simple approximate relations to permit easy visualization of the important limitations and potentialities of the device.

The analysis to this point has made minimum use of circuit considerations (except to note that logic devices require gain; this is because one output frequently has to control two or more inputs). A related logic circuit desideratum is that the component devices have at least three terminals since usually two different inputs control one output. It is difficult to adapt devices whose simplest form is of the two-terminal variety — as is the case for Gunn oscillators and tunnel diodes — to logic applications.

As in-depth discussion of materials is beyond the scope of this book, we have emphasized the importance of: (i) high limiting velocity v_s; (ii) high mobility μ and (iii) high breakdown field E_B, all three at high doping levels. Other important quantities are high thermal conductivity and low dielectric constant. Different device uses suggest different combinations of these quantities into "figures of merit", according to which different semiconductors may be and are compared. These comparisons moreover may be made as a function of temperature. (Lower than room temperature operation often looks attractive). When all is said and done, silicon remains the favorite material not because it has the highest figure of merit, although it does have a good one, but because it has the most controllable and reproducible materials technology. In particular its surface can form a more stable and controllable oxide (SiO_2) than most materials, and this oxide has proven invaluable in the passivation and processing technology of silicon devices.[26] Other potentially useful materials such as germanium, or gallium arsenide must demonstrate an equally reliable technology to prove competitive.

2.6 BISTABLE MEMORY DEVICES: AMORPHOUS SEMI-CONDUCTORS

Contrary to the impression that may have been generated by the preceding sections of this chapter, scientific understanding does not necessarily precede or even closely follow widespread technological interest in observed phenomena. Bistable semiconductor memory devices illustrate a notorious current example where such understanding is particularly lacking.

During the 1960's a number of quite different materials were found to possess two (or more) different resistance states, with varying degrees of permanence and reversibility in the electrical characteristics of the two states[27] (at least one example, MoS_2 dates back to 1923[28]). Some of the materials were amorphous thin films, examples being chalcogenide glasses[29] and Nb_2O_3, and it was soon realized that if the phenomenon could be demonstrated to be reproducible, rapid, and relatively free of degradation or fatigue problems, its use could improve both cost and performance characteristics of random access memories. Perhaps their application range could thereby be extended to mass storage.[27] These considerations led to substantial industrial research programs on switchable resistances. Despite these programs the underlying physics of the phenomena is still poorly understood. Indeed, at present, there appear to be almost as many suggested mechanisms as classes of materials exhibiting the effect, and in most cases there is still no agreement on the most probable mechanism for a particular material.

We shall focus our attention on the memory phenomenon schematically illustrated in Fig. 2-12. Electrodes are applied to a representative material in a processing sequence specific to the material, usually application of an initial "forming" current pulse. At this point the material is observed to be in the low-resistance, high-current state H. So long as operation is restricted to currents between A and D, it remains in this state. A current pulse of appropriate duration at A or D however switches the material to the high-resistance, low-current

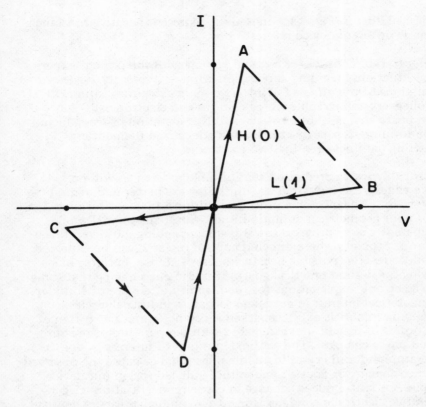

Figure 2-12. Simplified bistable resistance switching characteristics
showing high and low conductance states H and L,
identifiable as binary logic or memory O and 1 states,
respectively. The dashed regions are two possible
switching limits.

state L, where again it remains for voltages between B and C. An
appropriate voltage pulse (i.e., pulse from a relatively high imped-
ance source) in excess of C or D switches the material back to state
H.

This is an oversimplified and overgeneralized description. For some
materials the characteristic is symmetrical as shown, with switching
to either state possible in both quadrants I and III. For others it is
unsymmetrical, with say, H → L switching possible only in quadrant
I and L → H in quadrant III, (as shown). Also, the characteristics do
not retain complete linearity to the stability extreme A, B, C and D.

The dashed lines in Fig. 2-12, moreover, represent negative resistance regions of different device interest.

We refer to reference 27 for a recent summary of the present experimental situation, including application criteria. Presently suggested explanations of the effects fall into two main categories: thermally-controlled crystallographic phase changes and electronically-controlled phase changes. In most cases, the preparation process, including the forming step, seems to result in a localized filamentary conducting path between the two electrodes.

It is probably a safe prediction that bistable resistances will not achieve widespread industrial use until they are better understood theoretically. Reliance on a process requiring a filament-forming step of poor geometrical definition is also unsatisfactory. Despite the apparently slow progress towards understanding, however, this is the sort of problem where directed applied research can be expected to produce results (possible negative ones, of course, in terms of achieving the desired practical goal). It is also encouraging that some of the electronic explanations for the memory effect are of considerable theoretical interest in academic as well as industrial circles. Several bulk materials exhibit marked resistance variations (often of many orders of magnitude) associated with temperature or pressure-induced phase changes. The cardinal question of interest is, does a temperature-induced crystallographic phase change cause the observed resistance change, or does a temperature-induced (or, in our device examples, current-induced) change in carrier concentration trigger a cooperative electronic condensation to a much higher carrier density with little or no lattice deformation?[30] Alternatively, as in photochromic materials and MNOS transistors, are metastable long-lived electronic traps filled and emptied? This is one hypothesized mechanism for resistive bistability in semiconductor heterojunctions.[31] Just how is reversibility plus memory (i.e., controlled hysteresis) achieved? The expectation is that temperature-induced crystallographic changes will be inherently slow and subject to fatigue, but that electronically controlled ones may be both faster and more reliable. If such proves to be the case, eventually the resulting technology will be in debt to a school of pure theoretical research initiated in 1949 by N.F. Mott, for whom one class of such electronically induced metal-insulator phase changes is named.[29]

2.7 SUMMARY

An analysis of three types of integrated semiconductor devices — bipolar transistors, field-effect transistors, and charge-coupled devices — shows an increasing trend to utilization of thin surface layers of nearly homogeneous semiconductors. This minimizes processing complexity, and hence tends both to increase reliability and reduce cost — in some cases, at no expense in speed of electronic operation. In all cases, in silicon technology, power-time constant products can be minimized to the order of one picojoule. Understanding and control of surfaces is seen to assume increasing importance. The entrenched role of silicon technology can be understood to be largely a consequence of its ability to form a stable oxide. For cost-sensitive applications this entrenched role may be challenged by amorphous semiconductors or, more generally, two terminal bistable resistances. Another type of two-terminal device, the Gunn oscillator or amplifier, has achieved commercial importance in microwave circuits. A third materials technology, that of single crystal GaAs, is predominant here.

REFERENCES

1. K.E. Drangeid and R. Sommerhalder, "Dynamic Performance of Schottky-barrier Field-effect Transistors," *IBM J. Res. Develop. 14*, 82–94. (1970). See also Chapter 11, reference 26.

2. P. Wolf, "Microwave Properties of Schottky-barrier Field-effect Transistors" *ibid 14*, 125–141 (1970).

3. Th. O. Mohr, "Silicon and Silicon-dioxide Processing for High-frequency MESFET Preparation," *ibid 14*, 142–47 (1970).

4. W. Shockley, "A Unipolar Field-effect Transistor," *IRE 40*, 1365–76 (1952).

5. J.S. Lilienfeld, U.S. Pat. 1, 745,751 (1930), O. Heil, Brit. Pat. 439457 (Sept. 26, 1939). See also reference 10, Chapter 10.

6. J. Bardeen and W.H. Brattain, "The Transistor, A Semiconductor Triode", *Phys. Rev. 74*, 230–231 (1948); W. Shockley, "The Theory of p-n Junctions in Semiconductors and p-n Junction Transistors," *Bell System Tech. J. 28*, 435–489 (1949).

7. W. Shockley and G.L. Pearson, "Modulation of Conductance of Thin Films of Semiconductors by Surface Charges," *Phys. Rev. 74*, 232–233 (1948).

8. D. Frohman — Bentchkowsky, "The Metal-Nitride-Oxide-Silicon (MNOS) Transistor — Characteristics and Applications," *Proc. IEEE 58*, 1207–1219 (1970).

9. G.R. Brewer, "Electron and Ion Beams in Microelectronic Fabrication Processes," Solid State Technology *15*, (7), 36–39 and (8), 43–56 (1972). H.G. Dill, R.M. Finnlia, A.M. Leupp, T.N. Toombs, "The Impact of Ion

Implantation on Silicon Device and Circuit Technology," *ibid 15* (12), 27–35 (1972).

10.   A good recent text is S.M. Sze, "Physics of Semiconductor Devices," John Wiley and Sons, New York (1969).

11.   B.T. Murphy, V.J. Glinski, P.A. Gary, and R.A. Pedersen, "Collector Diffusion Isolated Integrated Circuits" *Proc. IEEE 57*, 1523–27 (1969).

12.   See, for example, W.S. Boyle and G.E. Smith, "Charge-coupled Devices — A new approach to MIS Device Structures," *IEEE Spectrum 8*, 18–27 (July 1971).

13.   The constant in this equation depends on both the space variation in the doping and on the injection level. We take here the case of high injection level, in which case the doping uniformity is relatively unimportant and 2 is the correct constant. See A.B. Phillips, *"Transistor Engineering"* (McGraw-Hill Book Co., New York, 1962), p. 243. For low injection level and uniform doping the constant is 1.

14.   M.F. Tompsett, G.F. Amelio, W.J. Bertram, Jr., R.G. Buckley, W.J. McNamara, J.C. Mikkelsen, Jr. and D.A. Sealer, "Charge-Coupled Imaging Devices: Experimental Results" *IEEE Trans. Electron Devices* ED — 8, 992–96 (1971).

15.   W.E. Engeler, J.J. Tiemann, and R.D. Baertsch, "Surface Charge Transport in Silicon" *Appl. Phys. Lett. 17*, 469–72 (1970).

16.   J.B. Gunn, "Microwave Oscillation of Current in III-V Semiconductors" *Solid State Commun. 1*, 88–91 (1963): "Instabilities of Current in III-V Semiconductors," *IBM J. Res. Develop. 8*, 141–151 (1964).

17.   B.K. Ridley and T.B. Watkins, "The Possibility of Negative Resistance Effects in Semiconductors," *Proc. Phys. Soc.* (London) 78, 293–304 (1961).

18.   H. Kroemer, "Theory of the Gunn Effect" *IEEE 52*, 1736 (1964).

19.   C. Hilsum, "Transferred Electron Amplifiers and Oscillators" *IRE 50*, 185–89 (1962).

20.   J.A. Copeland, "Stable Space Charge Layers in Two Valley Semi-conductors" *J. Appl. Phys. 37*, 3602–09 (1966).

21.   J.A. Copeland, "A New Mode of Operation for Bulk Negative Resistance Oscillators," *Proc. IEEE 54*, 1479–80 (1966).

22.   F. Sterzer, "Transferred Electron (Gunn) Amplifiers and Oscillators for Microwave Applications" *Proc. IEEE 59*, 1155–63 (1971).

23.   T. Sugeta, H. Yanai, and K. Sekido, "Schottky-Gate Bulk Effect Digital Devices" *Proc. IEEE 59*, 1629–30 (1971) and references there cited.

24. C. Hilsum and H.D. Rees, "Three-Level Oscillator: A New Form of Transferred Electron Device," *Electron. Lett. 6*, 277–278 (1970).

25. D. Colliver, C. Hilsum, B.D. Joyce, J.R. Morgan, and H.D. Rees, "Microwave Generation by InP 3-Level Transferred Electron Oscillators," *Electron Lett. 6*, 436 (1970).

26. See, for instance, A.S. Grove, "Physics and Technology of Semiconductor Devices," John Wiley and Sons, New York (1967).

27. See, for instance, R.E. Matick, "Review of Current Proposed Technologies for Mass Storage Systems," *Proc. IEEE 60*, 266–89 (1972) and references contained therein.

28. A.T. Waterman, "The Electrical Conductivity of Molybdenite," *Rev. 21*, 540–49 (1923).

29. N.F. Mott, "The Basis of the Electron Theory of Metals with Special Reference to the Transition Metal is " *Proc. Soc.* (London)*A62*, 416–22 (1949), "The Transition to the Metallic State," *Phil. Mag. 6*, 287–304 (1961).

30   S.R. Ovshinsky, "Reversible Electrical Switching Phenomena in Disordered Structures," *Phys. Rev. Lett. 21*, 1450–53 (1968).

31. H.J. Hovel, "Switching and Memory in ZnSe-Ge Heterojunctions," *Appl. Phys. Lett. 17*, 141–43 (1970).

PROBLEMS

2.1 In Fig. 2-1, assume that the depletion layer is $0.1\,\mu m$ thick and that the time constant for charge leakage from the insulated gate is determined by the residual resistivity of this layer.

a.   What is the equivalent circuit of the floating gate?

b.   What resistivity is required for a time constant of one second? Of one month?

c.   In b, what is the carrier density required in the conduction band ($\mu = 500$ cm^2/V) for the above time constants? What carrier densities would be involved if a lower mobility of 0.5 cm^2/V prevailed (perhaps corresponding to "hopping" conductivity of shallow trapped charge carriers?

2.2 One of the answers of 2-1 c is $N \cong 10^4$/cm^3. Assume that the leakage charges are available from thermal excitation across the valence band, $N_v \cong 10^{19}$/cm^3 and the Boltzman distribution of mobile charge

N prevails ($N/N_v = e^{-eV/kT}$ where V is the depth in volts of the trapped charge reservoir below the conduction of hopping band).

a.   For room temperature — $300°K$ — what value of E corresponds to the required $N/N_v = 10^{-15}$? How does this compare with the energy band gap of silicon?

b.   By how large a factor is the time constant increased by operating at $77°K$?

2.3   Look up the materials characteristics of GaAs epitaxial films at room temperature (Willardson and Beer, "Semiconductors and Semi-metals," Volume 7, Academic Press, 1971). Assuming the same device dimensions as those for the Silicon FET of Eq. (2-6).

a.   What is the optimum doping level?

b.   What is the power dissipation per unit volume at this doping level?

c.   What is the time constant?

d.   What is the figure of merit?

2.4   An experimental 256 bit charge coupled device shift register shows a charge transfer efficiency of 99.96% per bit at 100 kilohertz operations. (N.A. Patrin, IBM, J. Research Development *17*, 241 1973.)

a.   What is the overall transfer efficiency at the end of the shift register?

b.   At 4 MHz, operation of the overall transfer efficiency of a comparable 128 bit device is reduced to 50%. What is the corresponding charge transfer efficiency per bit?

c.   What is the physical principle underlying "fat zero" operation, and by how much does it improve overall transfer efficiency at 4 MHz?

2.5   What electron temperature is necessary if 50% of the electrons in a GaAs Gunn oscillator are transferred to the higher energy band. Assume a Boltzman distribution, $N_u/(N_u + N_L) = e^{-eV/kT}$.

Magnetic Information Storage

Recent advances in device concepts and materials technology have
led to new systems concepts in magnetic information storage. The
possible use of continuous magnetic surfaces, already familiar in
magnetic tapes and disks, have been extended to stationary media
with movable magnetization states ("magnetic bubbles") and to
optical writing and reading of magnetic information (thermo-magneto-
optic memories or beam-addressable files). In contrast to semiconductor technology, where several different devices can be optimized
by one material (silicon), with magnetic phenomena each device
principle leads to a different optimization of material parameters.

From the point of view of the computer industry, the primary important magnetic phenomenon is that of permanent but easily alterable
remnant magnetization in ferromagnetic and ferrimagnetic materials.
This phenomenon is extensively used in magnetic storage — primarily,
for our purposes, of a bistable digital type, although analog storage
of a range of remnant magnetization states is also important. We
shall develop the theme of technologically important magnetic
phenomena around the central point of bistable, erasable storage.

3.1 MAGNETIC BUBBLE DEVICES

Both because of the current technological interest in the subject
and the clarity of the physics involved, we introduce our discussion
of magnetic phenomena and devices in a unconventional fashion, starting with a completely integrated structure utilizing the phenomenon
of "magnetic bubbles".[1] Magnetic bubble devices are one outgrowth
of basic materials research programs on the properties of magnetic
domains. When thin sections of certain semi-transparent single-
crystal magnetic crystals were examined optically by a polarizing
microscope, the domain structure was clearly revealed by the different rotation angles for plane-polarized light (hence different optical
transmission through the analyzer) of domains with different magnet-

ization directions.[2 -4]   In some cases the preferred magnetization
directions were perpendicular to the plane of the sheet and, in zero
magnetic field, consisted of many narrow, oppositely directed domains, leaving the net magnetization of the sheet zero.   Furthermore,
and the point of practical interest, in the presence of an appropriately
chosen biasing magnetic field perpendicular to the sheet, energetically
unfavorably-oriented domains do not disappear, but shrink in size
and assume a circular shape[3 ,4] (Fig. 3-1).   It is these small cylinders
of reverse magnetization that are referred to as "magnetic bubbles".
The first step towards practical devices utilized thin single crystal
layers of magnetic materials grown epitaxially on non-magnetic
substrates.[5]   More recently, thin films of some amorphous magnetic
materials have also been tailored to exhibit favorable magnetic bubble
properties, thus raising hopes of more economic fabrication.[6]

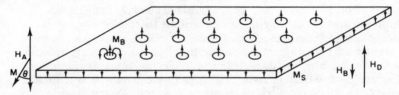

Figure 3-1.   Magnetic bubbles. In a thin sheet of unixial magnetic
          material a stable two-phase system exists (for suffic-
          iently large uniaxial anisotropy H_A and a range of bias-
          ing fields H_B) in which a minority phase of cylindrical
          domains of one magnetization is uniformly dispersed in
          the majority phase of the opposite magnetization (formed
          by H_B). The demagnetization field H_D of the majority
          phase stabilizes the minority phase.

As is often the case, a time lag ensued before the original observations
were recognized to be directly related to new device concepts (actually, in this case, already evolving along a different path),[1] rather
than indirectly related to interpreting existing device properties.
Before describing these concepts, let us review the magnetostatic
energy balance in the above-described thin sheet in order to better
understand the phenomenon.

To begin with, the fact that the domain magnetization, in zero external field, lies preferentially in a direction perpendicular to the
plane poses a constraint on the relation between the intrinsic anistropy
of the material (the forces tending to align the magnetization along
a particular crystallographic or growth direction), the piezomagnetic
anistropy (there may be a stress field related to the surface layer

which will also tend to orient the magnetization), and the shape anistropy of the sheet (the demagnetizing field $H_D = 4\pi M_s$ will tend to align the magnetization M_s in the plane of the sheet). For our purposes, and in the materials of present interest, we can lump together these several anistropies into a single uniaxial anistropy in the direction perpendicular to the plane of the sheet, with an energy density $K \sin^2 \theta$ where θ is the angle between the magnetization and the normal to the plane. The magnetization energy is $-\vec{H}_D \cdot \vec{M}_s$. Hence the condition for a stable equilibrium at $\theta = 0$ is

$$\frac{\partial}{\partial \theta} (K \sin^2 \theta + 4\pi M_s^2 \cos\theta) = \left[(2K\cos\theta - 4\pi M_s^2) \sin\theta \right]_{\theta=0} = 0$$

$$\frac{\partial^2}{\partial \theta^2} (K \sin^2 \theta + 4\pi M_s^2 \cos\theta) = \left[(2K\cos\theta - 4\pi M_s^2) \cos\theta - 2K \sin^2 \theta \right]_{\theta=0} > 0$$

or $(H_A + H_D) M_s > 0$ \hfill (3-1)

where, in analogy to H_D, we have defined an anistropy field H_A as $H_A = 2K/M_s$. Thus Eq. (3-1) alternatively can be written as

$$K > 2\pi M_s^2 \hfill (3-2)$$

or

$$H_A > 4\pi M_s$$

with

$$K/2\pi M_s^2 = Q > 1 \hfill (3-3)$$

specifying the factor by which the inequality (3-2) is satisfied. When this inequality is fulfilled, the stable magnetization condition of the sheet in zero-applied magnetic field is indeed one where the local magnetization direction is perpendicular to the plane of the sheet. More detailed analysis balances the short range exchange forces favoring aligned magnetic moments with the long range magnetostatic forces favoring a reversed magnetization arising from the return loop of the magnetic flux at a position distant from the local magnetization. As a result, the magnetic pattern breaks up as described above, with the boundaries between the regions of opposite magnetization formed by "domain walls" with a complicated spiral magnetic transition region. The size of the domains and the bias field region in which they assume a circular shape, are determined in part by the shape dependence of the demagnetizing field.[8]

It is evident that the above-described phenomena are the result of a subtle balance of forces or energies. Consequently they are easily disturbed by the imposition of further weak external forces. For example, a magnetized needle brought near the plane will move the bubbles around. Thus an appropriate time-and-distance-varying magnetic field can be designed to move the bubbles from place to place. It is also a considerable simplification in these devices that the bubbles tend to repel one another — a consequence of the effects of the demagnetizing fields. These fundamental magnetostatic considerations — simple in concept although somewhat complicated in mathematical detail — have led to a family of integrated magnetic devices which, as with the charge-coupled semiconductor devices (Chapter 2), we shall shortly illustrate by a shift-register example. As in the semiconductor case, we must add some dynamic concepts, too, which we shall do with a somewhat phenomenological argument involving "viscous" damping of the wall motion.[7] Consider the decrease in magnetic energy that takes place when a domain of favored orientation is expanded a distance ∂x in field H parallel to the magnetization. This is

$$\partial E = 2M_s H \partial A \partial x = F_H \, \partial x \tag{3-4}$$

where F_H is the force on an element of area ∂A of the domain wall which moves the distance ∂x. The opposing viscous drag force F_D is assumed to be proportional to the magnetization, the velocity, and ∂A. Choosing the constant of proportionality as in Eq. (3-5).

$$F_D = 2M_s V \partial A / \mu \tag{3-5}$$

gives

$$V = \mu H, \tag{3-6}$$

thus defining a domain wall mobility μ.

At low drive fields a linear proportionality of v to H is indeed found, but, particularly in high-mobility materials (some garnets, for example), the velocity is found to saturate at high fields, a phenomenon reminiscent of the saturated drift velocity of charge carriers in semiconductors. According to one theory,[9] this saturated velocity, v_s, is given by

$$v_s = 7.1\gamma \, A d^{-1} K^{-1/2} \tag{3-7}$$

where γ is the gyromagnetic ratio, or precession frequency of a free electron spin per unit magnetic field

$$\gamma = 1.76 \times 10^7 \ \sec^{-1}/\text{gauss} \tag{3-8}$$

A is the exchange energy of the magnetic material, and d is the thickness of film.

Let us return to the actual device. More detailed magnetostatic analysis leads to an interrelation between the optimum, or "preferred" value d_p, and the magnetization which, according to Thiele[8] is given by

$$d_p = r_p = 4\ell \tag{3-9}$$

where

$$\ell = (AK)^{1/2}/\pi M_s^2$$

If we add the restriction of Eq. (3-3) a "preferred" value of ℓ, $\ell = \ell_p$, is

$$\ell_p = 2Q(A/K)^{1/2} = 2Q\,\delta\,/\pi \tag{3-10}$$

where

$$\delta = \pi(A/K)^{1/2} \tag{3-11}$$

is the width of the domain walls.[7]

Substituting Eqs. (3-9) and (3-10) into Eq. (3-7) gives a value for v_s, when dimensions are optimized, which is independent of d or K:

$$v_s = 0.89\gamma \ Q^{-1} A^{1/2} \ \text{cm/sec} \tag{3-12}$$

The exchange constant A does not vary much among materials with a usefully high Curie temperature.

$$A = 4 \times 10^{-7} \ \text{ergs/cm} \tag{3-13}$$

is a value fairly typical of magnetic insulators. Eq. (3-12) thus becomes

$$v_s \cong 10^4 \ Q^{-1} \ \text{cm/sec} \tag{3-14}$$

a surprisingly materials-independent quantity. We see also that there is a trade-off between maximum speed of bubble propagation and stability of the domains in the dependence of these quantities on Q.

Returning now to Eq. (3-9) we note that for a fixed choice of ℓ and d, a range of values of r, and of spacings between the bubbles, as a function of H exists over which this uniform dispersion of a minor "bubble" phase in the major magnetization phase is stable.[8] Equally important, the phase with no reversed bubbles, or intermediate phases with one or a few reversed bubbles is metastable and strongly so. It takes the surmounting of a considerable nucleation energy to form a bubble if the bubble domain state is approached from the region of high bias field where the sample is completely magnetized in one direction. The essence of a shift-register device design then is the following. First choose a structure which satisfies relations (3-2) and (3-9) and which is of the desired bubble radius (small, perhaps 1 μm). Then design some periodic (in space) magnetic-field variation which will trap individual bubbles in preferred locations. Finally, and simultaneously, add to the design a feature whereby a periodic (in time) variation in the magnetic field will move the bubble progressively — in a preferred direction — from one trapping site to another. This is, and has been, the subject of invention. Fig. 3-2 shows one such embodiment:[1] an added permalloy "T and I bar" overlay to Fig. 3-1. If to the plane-normal bias field H_B is added an in-plane component which is cyclically rotated, one can convince oneself that the trapped bubble position moves to the right as shown.

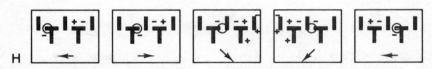

Figure 3-2.   T and I bar bubble device. A rotating bias horizontal magnetic field (black arrows) magnetizes an overlay of permalloy T and I strips as indicated by the magnetic + and − dipoles. The circular magnetic bubble has the minus end of its dipole adjacent to the overlay. Magnetostatic attraction traps the bubble and moves it along cyclically as shown.

The preceding analysis may sound complicated, but it is actually less phenomenological than that required for understanding the statics and dynamics of the bistable magnetic switching which we shall discuss shortly. It is true that the latter can be described without direct reference to crystalline anistropy. On the other hand, we have not had to use the concepts of coercive field and remnant magnetization or the rather mysterious material requirements of a square magnetization loop. Moreover, the end result, an integrated device with movable magnetic regions, is an excellent example of desirable planar technology. (These devices do have to cope with a materials-related coercive field that represents a threshold for domain motion. However this is essentially a consequence of material and surface imperfections which can be reduced to acceptable values by proper processing.) As with charge-coupled devices, special techniques are required to initiate and detect the bubble motion. We shall not discuss the sensing devices, which are variants of conventional magnetic-field sensing devices.

Let us now seek to maximize our packing density and transfer rate, which can be done simultaneously by minimizing the bubble size since v_s is independent of d. We choose

$$r_p = d_p = 1\mu m$$

$$\ell_p = 0.25\mu m \tag{3-15}$$

We shall also pick as a reasonable trade-off value between speed and stability:

$$Q = 5$$

$$v_s = 2,000 \text{ cm/sec} \tag{3-16}$$

Hence, from Eq. (3-14)

$$R = \tau^{-1} = v_s/8r_p = 2.5 \text{ megabits per second (Mbs)}$$

where τ is the transfer time — or R the data rate — to complete a cycle of four bubble diameters in Fig. 3-2. Experimental bubble transfer rates in a number of different structures and different materials cover a range between 0.1 and 1 Mbs.[10]

From Eqs. (3-10), (3-13) and (3-15) then

$$K = 64,000 \text{ ergs/cm}^3 \tag{3-17}$$

whence, by Eqs. (3-2) and (3-3)

$$M_s = 45 \text{ gauss}$$

$$4\pi M_s = 570 \text{ gauss} \tag{3-18}$$

$$H_A = 2850 \text{ gauss}$$

Figure 3-3 shows a graph of some typical material properties with the prescription of Eqs. (3-18) indicated by 'x' ($4\pi M_s$ = "magnetization") located in the "preferred-materials" area. Since material properties can be altered over continuous broad ranges by varying composition (and stress, not indicated as a parameter in the figure), a variety of materials, many of the garnet type, approach this optimum region and can be further optimized with respect to mobility and coercive field H_c.

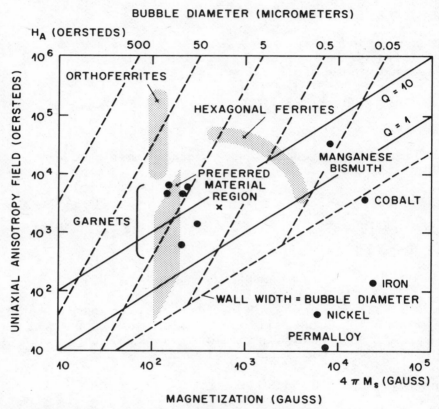

Figure 3-3. Magnetic bubbles materials. Stability of magnetic bubbles requires $Q = H_A/4\pi M_s > 1$. High limiting bubble velocity requires low Q. Reasonable miniaturization and Q = 5 dictates preferred materials near x marks. Garnets fall close to this region. Adapted from reference 1.

With the aid of the preceding relations, we may also estimate the work expended in moving a bubble. Let us assume that the viscous drag on a bubble of radius r and thickness d is equivalent to that on two walls (front and back of the bubble) each of cross section 2 r d — i.e., that the effective wall area is the projection of the cylindrical wall. Then the work done in moving the bubble, say four diameters, at is maximum velocity v_s is

$$W = F_D \times 4 \, rd \times 8r = 64 \, M_s \, v_s \, dr^2 / \mu \qquad (3\text{-}19)$$

where, as in Chapter 2, we assume that we operate at the knee of the v-field curve so that both the relations $v = v_s$ and $v = \mu H$ are approximately valid. It is difficult to relate the mobility to material parameters,[11] but in a number of garnet materials near the preferred region a value

$$\mu \cong 1,000 \text{ cm/sec} - \text{Oe} \qquad (3\text{-}20)$$

is attainable.[9,10] Together with the magnitudes of Eqs. (3-15), (3-16) and (3-18), this gives a transfer energy of

$$E = 5.8 \times 10^{-9} \text{ ergs} = 5.8 \times 10^{-4} \text{ picojoules}, \qquad (3\text{-}21)$$

a value several orders of magnitude smaller than that required in the competitive charge-coupled semiconductor technology (which has, however, shorter time constants and, for relatively small arrays, can be integrated with other semiconductor devices using the same technology). Figure 3-4 shows two experimental structures indicating the fabrication and bit density trends of bubble devices. Essentially perfect memory chips as large as 20K bit have been reported.[12]

3.2 EARLIER FORMS OF MAGNETIC STORAGE

The more traditional forms of magnetic storage include cores, disks, tape, and magnetic film. The phenomena involved in all these examples are best described with reference to the familiar hysteresis loop of a finite sample of magnetic material (Fig. 3-5). We shall think of this loop first as applying to a magnetic core, or toroid, for which shape the demagnetizing factor is very small. Hence the plot directly shows the magnetization as a function of the applied field. After an initial portion dependent on the history of the sample (here shown starting from zero magnetization) a symmetrical, repeatable curve develops. The physical process of magnetization reversal involves both rotation and growth of magnetic domains in a more involved fashion than for magnetic bubbles.[7]

The bistable magnetic storage states are those which $H = 0$ and $M = \pm M_r$, the remnant magnetization. For the square hysteresis loop typical of good magnetic core materials, $M_r \approx M_s$.

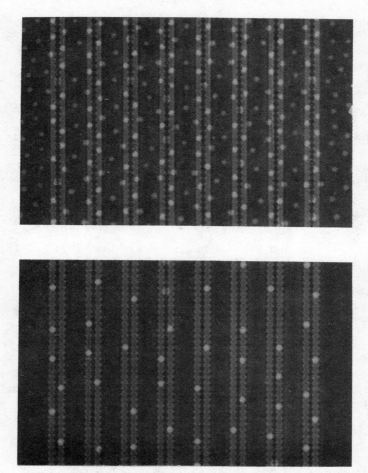

Figure 3-4A. 6μm wide bubble tracks produced by photolithographic process on a garnet film covered, except for the track locations, with a 2,000 Å film of Si. Reproduced from R.L. LeCraw et al., ref. 10, with permission of the authors. The white circles are the bubbles.

The work done in switching from one state to the other is half the hysteresis loop area, i.e., for a square loop

$$p\tau = 2H_c M_s \text{ ergs/cm}^3 \qquad (3\text{-}22)$$

where H_c is the coercive field. Typical value of H_c and M_s for Mg-Mn

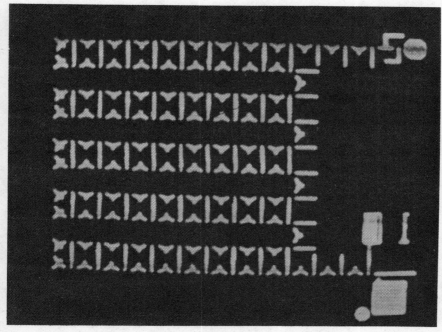

Figure 3-4B. A 100 bit shift register[12] with 0.4 μm linewidth and a density of 10^6 bit/cm^2. Reproduced from ref. 12 with permission of the authors.

and Li-Mn ferrites,[14] materials used in magnetic cores are

$$H_c = 2 \text{ oersteds} \tag{3-23}$$

$$M_s = 100 \text{ gauss}$$

for which $P_T = 4 \times 10^{-5}$ picojoules per cubic micron. A typical small core might have an outer diameter of 20 mils and an inner diameter of 10 mils for a volume of $\approx 10^7$ (μm)^3 for a 400 picojoule switching energy.

Magnetic cores are usually organized in planar arrays with "read" and "write" wires threading through the cores. Fig. (1-2B) Currents passing through the write wires establish the proper magnetization state. When this results in switching a core, the induced current is picked up on the read wire, thus reading the initial state of the core. Without going into the details of the organization, a sequence of bits corresponding to a word can be read out at one time over a particular read wire, etc. Writing is often accomplished by a matrix addressing

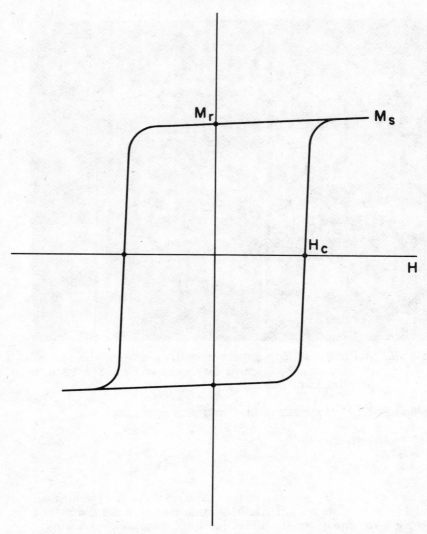

Figure 3-5.   Square hysteresis loop. Some magnetically soft materials (low coercive field H_c) with low shape-demagnetizing fields (cylindrical closed-loop cores or flat films) have nearly square magnetization loops. The remnant magnetization M_r nearly equals the saturation magnetization M_s.

with each bit threaded by two orthogonal wires in such a fashion that simultaneous write pulses exceed the coercive field and switch the bit, whereas single pulses do not. We see that if each core in such an array could be made as small as our magnetic bubble example (a volume of $\pi \ \mu m^3$), its switching energy would be less than the work done in moving a magnetic bubble. However, this is clearly not a feasible structure. Hence the search for a more easily integrated device.

The value of H_c quoted for magnetic cores is that of a magnetically "soft" material, where easy magnetization reversal is desired and operation in an environment free of stray magnetic fields is possible. Magnetic-tape storage operates in a different mode. Here a coating of fine magnetic particles (thin metallic films are also used) is applied to a flexible substrate material. The tape is transported at high speed under a fixed reading and writing head where localized magnetization bits are written in the plane of the tape by current pulses through

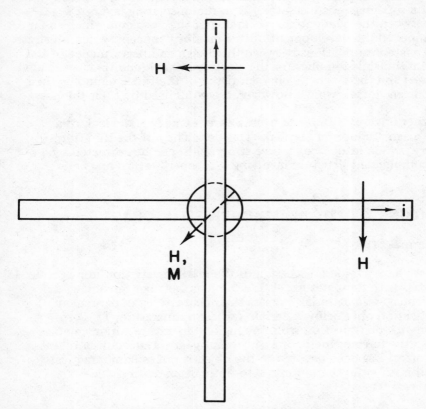

Figure 3-6. Thin-film memory element. Coincident current pulses in orthogonal transmission lines switch thin-film magnetization in direction shown.

a coil in the write head. Here we do have a continuous recording medium, but at the price of mechanical transport of the data. We shall not pursue this subject further except to note that "harder" magnetic materials are required, with higher coercive fields, so that the stray fields of adjacent bits, perhaps on the next tape layer on a spool, will not switch the bits.

Finally, we note that the matrix switching configuration of magnetic cores has also been investigated for thin magnetic films. Wires threading through magnetic cores are replaced by thin disks of magnetic films at the intersections between crossed arrays of thin-film electrical conductors,[14] thus forming a planar structure (Fig. 3-6) which indeed can be fabricated so as to have a fairly small volume of magnetic bit to be switched (typically 10^2 x 10^2 x $1 = 10^4$ μm^3). The coercive field of a soft magnetic alloy such as permalloy is even lower than that of a soft magnetic insulator. Thin-film insulating layers are used between the conductors. A catalog of the problems which so far have impeded the development of this memory concept would illustrate the intimate interrelations between the design and performance of the thin-film transmission lines for the electrical signal (and their associated IR losses) and the magnetic characteristics of the films, including their eddy-current losses, which, however, are minimized by their thinness.

One other obvious difference from a core memory is the lack of a closed magnetic loop in Fig. 3-6. This deficiency of the thin-film memory, which leads to excessive stray fields, can be corrected by a more complicated structure involving a "keeper" return magnetic path.

3.3 MAGNETO-OPTIC BEAM-ADDRESSED STORAGE

a. Thermal Effects

So far we have avoided discussion of the marked variation in magnetic properties with temperature. It is a familiar fact that ferromagnetic and ferrimagnetic materials possess their characteristic permanent magnetization only below a certain critical temperature, T_c, corresponding to the transition from the high-temperature paramagnetic phase to the ferromagnetic one. In recent years, a substantial research effort has been devoted to the objective of making practical use of this effect in thermo-magneto-optic beam-addressable memories.[15]

Consider the magnetization vs. temperature and coecive field vs. temperature plots of Fig. 3-7. The principle of thermo-magnetic writing is to start with a magnetic thin film with a uniform satur-

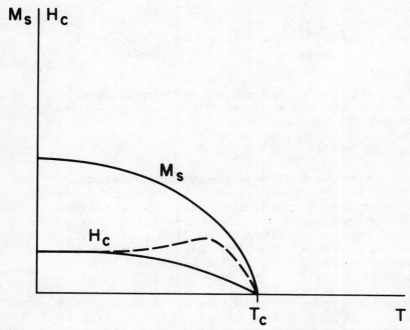

Figure 3-7. Temperature dependence of H_c and M_s. The saturation
magnetization M_s and coercive field H_c both vanish
above the Curie temperature T_c; however, in general,
they obey different temperature laws. In neither case is
the function necessarily a monotonically decreasing one.

ated magnetization M_s (T_1), and coercive field H_c(T_1). Depending
on the material anistropy, M may be either in the plane of the film
or perpendicular to it. This film is then placed in a biasing field
H_B < H_c in a direction opposing the magnetization. Since H_B < H_c
the film will not switch its magnetization direction.

A small spot of radius r of the film is now heated rapidly, as by a
pulse of laser light incident on the film, to a temperature T_2 > T_c.
When the spot cools, which it also does very rapidly because of its
small size, it will become remagnetized in the reverse direction to that
of the rest of the film. Thus a magnetic bit is written. The history
of optical observation of magnetic domains[2-4] makes it obvious that
it can also be read optically, making use of the Faraday effect.

Let us now make some numerical estimates. We shall assume that
the heating is sufficiently rapid that the temperature rise is determined
by the specific heat alone. Then the writing energy density is

$$E_w = \int_{T_1}^{T_2} (C_M + C_{NM}) \, dT = (E_{M1} - E_{M2}) + C_{NM} (T_2 - T_1)$$

$$(3\text{-}24)$$

where C_M and C_M are the magnetic and nonmagnetic parts of the specific heat per unit volume, respectively. The magnetic exchange energy density E_M is given by

$$E_M = 1/2 \, H_M \cdot M_s \qquad\qquad (3\text{-}25)$$

where H_M is the molecular field (typically about 10^7 oersteds).[14] E_{M2} is zero if the film is heated above T_c. In this case E_M per unit volume exceeds the switching energy of previous examples by a factor ranging from $H_M/4H_c$ to $H_M \mu/40 \, v_s$, i.e., by up to a factor of 10^6 at room temperature. A typical example is a CrTe film[15] for which $M_s = 80$ and $H_c = 117$ oersteds at room temperature and $T_c = 61°C$. For such a film $E_m = 40$ picojoules/$\mu m^3 = 10$ calories/cm^3.

The required temperature rise determines the contribution from the nonmagnetic specific heat, assuming an average value of about 0.5 calories/cm^3 (a value nearly independent of the material). In the above example it would require a $20°$ temperature rise for the non-magnetic contribution to equal the magnetic one. However, variants on the above scheme exist for which the required magnetic energy change is much less. In fact, in one variant (reorientation writing)[16] the parameter that changes with temperature is the anistropy direction, and the magnetization changes hardly at all. Hence, we shall rather arbitrarily assume that a value of E_w to be compared to other devices is given by a $50°C$ temperature rise, using the nonmagnetic specific heat, i.e.,

$$E_w = 100 \text{ picojoules}/\mu m^3 \qquad\qquad (3\text{-}26)$$

For a typical film thickness of 0.1 μm an alternative measure is 10 picojoules per μm^2. This figure may be reduced by a factor of ten or more by operation at cryogenic temperatures.[15] Allowance for heat conductivity and reflection losses will raise the required laser pulse energy above this minimum figure.

We note that the material design requirements on H_c for this mode of switching differ significantly for those for magnetic bubbles and magnetic cores. For the latter material, H_c was desired to be as small as possible (consistent in the later case with a square hysteresis loop). In the magneto-thermal case, we must localize the magnetic bits, i.e., we must optimize the coercivity rather than minimize it. Specifically, we must satisfy the inequality[17']

$$H_c > |H_w + H_D| = | \frac{2(AK)^{1/2}}{M_s r} | + H_D \qquad (3-27)$$

where H_w is the domain-wall surface tension tending to collapse the spot, and H_D the demagnetizing field tending to expand it. Thus

$$r > \frac{2(AK)^{1/2}}{M_s(H_c - H_D)} \qquad (3-28)$$

where H_D is equal to zero for M_s parallel to the plane. The assumption $H_D = 0$ always overestimates r if M_s is normal to the film, but is a good approximation if $r \gg d$ and $H_D \ll 4\pi M_s$.

H_c is a particularly phenomenological quantity, difficult to relate to more basic quantities. If, for example, our thin film behaves like an aggregate of fine uniaxial particles with a multidomain structure, one theoretical estimate[14] is

$$H_c \approx 0.2 \, H_A = 0.2 \, K/M_s \qquad (3-29)$$

Such an estimate, for a material with the parameters of Eqs. (3-13), (3-15) and (3-18), and with $H_D = 0$, would give $H_c = 285$ oersteds and $r > 0.25 \, \mu m$. For CrTe, assuming $A = 4 \times 10^{-7}$ ergs/cm, $r > 1.1$ μm. These values are of the order of magnitude observed for thermo-magnetic writing. Indeed, for MnBi even smaller domains have been written, allowing thermo-magnetic recording of holograms, i.e., magneto-optic gratings with periodicities of the order of the wavelength of light.[18,19] Such holograms are also embodiments of thermo-magneto-optic storage.[18] (Some aspects of holographic storage are discussed in Chapters 1 and 4).

b. Optical Effects

As already noted, the magnetization direction of a small magnetic sample, for instance, a magnetic bubble or magneto-thermally written spot in a thin film, can be sensed by the rotation in the plane of polarization of a light beam transmitted through the sample (if somewhat transparent) or reflected from it. The physical effects involved are known, respectively, as the Faraday effect, F, and the magnetic Kerr effect. If thus becomes a problem of technological interest to be able to estimate these quantities and to relate them to the optical absorption of the materials.

In insulators, the Faraday effect is essentially a consequence of the anomalous refractive index changes in the vicinity of an absorption line or band. The simplest situations[20] are shown in Fig. 3-8. In Fig. 3-8A the ferromagnetic ground state is connected to the excited state of interest by allowed right circularly polarized radiation only (with respect to the internal magnetic field). In Fig. 3-8B it is connected to the two levels of an excited state doublet, split by $2h\Delta$, by right polarized radiation to the upper doublet and left to the lower. The corresponding absorption and anomalous dispersion are shown in Figs. 3-8C and 3-8D.

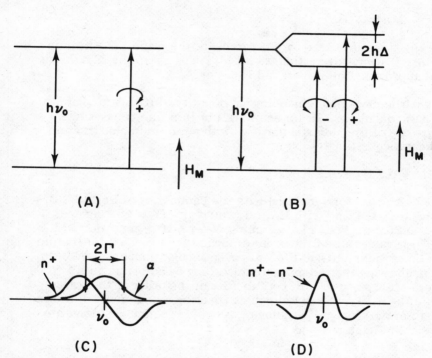

Figure 3-8.   Faraday rotation. A) An allowed transition for right circularly polarized radiation only (+) with respect to H_M in the ferromagnetic state. B) Allowed left circularly polarized radiation (–) to the lower doublet of an excited state split by $2h\Delta$, and right (+) to the upper state. C) The dispersion-line shape for n^+ corresponding to 8A and the corresponding absorption α, of line width 2Γ. D) The difference between the refractive index dispersion curves for n^+ and n^-, separated in frequency by 2Δ, corresponding to 8B. Adapted from reference 20.

In a material exhibiting circular birefringence, as above, an incident linear polarized light beam is better described as a superposition of two circularly polarized beams of opposite rotation. These beams travel at different velocities in their passage through the medium, and hence develop a relative phase shift. When the circularly polarized beams are recombined on leaving the material, the plane of polarization is rotated by half the phase shift. This is the Faraday rotation. (There is also some dispersion in the absorption, hence the amplitudes of the exciting circularly polarized beams are unequal, and they actually recombine to an elliptically polarized wave of small minor axis. We shall ignore this.)

The intimate relation of absorption to refractive index dispersion in Figs. 3-8C and 3-8D enables one to relate the maximum Faraday rotation, F_M, to the absorption constant α *rising from the transition discussed* by figures of merit:

$$F_M/\alpha = \frac{1}{4} \text{ radians} \tag{3-30A}$$

or

$$F_M/\alpha = \frac{\Delta}{4\Gamma} \text{ radians} \tag{3-30B}$$

for the cases of Figs. 3-8A and 3-8B, respectively, where it is assumed that $\Delta << \Gamma$. In Eq. (3-30A), the maximum in F occurs at a frequency offset of Γ, the line half-width, from the center of the transition, but in Eq. (3-30B) it occurs at the line center.

Most ferromagnetic materials depart widely from the models of Figs. 3-8 and Eqs. (3-30). The multiplet structure of the transitions is more complicated (and often unknown). More serious, the optical absorption often arises from different, stronger transitions than those that determine the Faraday rotation. Consequently, the figures of merit are generally much poorer than one would deduce from Eqs. (3-30). An exception is EuO, with $T_c = 77°K$, whose Faraday rotation line shape and other spectroscopic evidence suggest applicability of the model of Fig. 3-8B.[17] At 5°K, F_M and α peak at a wavelength of 0.7 μm, with values of 5×10^5 degrees cm^{-1} and 8×10^4 cm^{-1}, respectively,[21] for $F_M/\alpha = 6.3°$ or 0.11 radians. This implies an effective Δ/Γ of 0.4. The large values of F and α also imply nearly allowed optical transitions (strong line strength f, of approximately 0.1).

One would prefer, of course, to work with magnetic materials with Curie temperatures above room temperature. This requires that the

primary magnetic ion be a 3d transition element rather than a 4f rare
earth. Much remains to be done in optimizing the magneto-optical
properties of these materials. Furthermore, metallic alloys, for which
the theoretical approach is somewhat different from that outlined
above, are also candidates for practical application. An example is
MnBi,[22] with T_c = 360°C, and the convenient property of the easy
magnetic axis normal to the plane of the film. (It lies in the plane
of the film for EuO.) For MnBi at room temperature and λ = 0.63
μm, f = 5.4 x 10^5 degrees cm^{-1} and α = 3.8 x 10^5 cm^{-1}, for F/α =
1.42°.

The above discussion has emphasized maximizing F, as is required
for thin-film applications and high spatial resolution of memory
spots. For other applications one may wish to maximize F/α, which
can be done by working at an optical frequency far removed from
resonance. The more general relation for Fig. 3-8A is

$$F/\alpha = \frac{\nu_0 - \nu}{4\Gamma} \qquad\qquad (3\text{-}31)$$

Thus, for yttrium iron garnet at 1.2 μm and 300°K,[23] F = 240°cm^{-1},
α = 0.069 cm^{-1}, F/α = 3500°.

3.4   MAGNETIC MATERIALS AND THE PHYSICS OF MAGNETISM

It is much more difficult to separate materials-related questions from
a discussion of magnetic phenomena than is the case with semiconductors. In the latter case, we were able to illustrate most of the
central phenomena by discussing one material, silicon, which at
present is overwhelmingly more important technologically than any
other semiconductor. Such is not the case with magnetic materials.
Even restricting the discussion to magnetic storage, such widely different substances as metallic alloys (permalloy), powders of hard
magnetic oxides (for magnetic tape or disks) and soft ferrites (for
cores) are commercially important today, and still different materials
loom on the horizon for magnetic bubbles and thermo-magneto-
optical memories. Moreover, few useful magnetic materials are as
pure as even highly-doped silicon. Rather, they consist of alloys and
mixed compounds, often of substances of considerable complexity
even in their pure form. Thus the microscopic details of magnetic
phenomena are indeed very materials-related. Among the simplest
generalizations that may help one limit the range of materials of
industrial interest is that for useful room-temperature properties the
primary magnetic ion must be a member of the 3d transition group.
(The exchange interactions in the 4f series are too weak, resulting in

a low Curie temperature). Of course, one may always find that technological trade-offs eventually favor operation of some devices or systems at cryogenic temperatures; in this case the range of potentially useful materials is much wider. To date, the normal research-and-development trend, however, has often been to explore a potentially attractive technological phenomenon at cryogenic temperatures (if its properties are optimum there) and then find ways to develop alternative materials in which the phenomenon works satisfactorily at room temperatures.

Besides the specificity of materials to application, magnetism differs from electrical conduction in several other important aspects. The absence of free magnetic charge is one central point which, of course, is embodied in the theory at an early stage. Perhaps even more fundamental, permanent magnetic phenomena are intrinsically cooperative in nature. They result from many-body effects. An isolated magnetic dipole-spin possesses none of the attributes of ferromagnetism, whereas an isolated electronic charge is the basic unit of electrical conduction, with an intrinsic mobility only secondarily modified by many-body effects. Hence, size and shape effects already noted to be important in semiconductor phenomena are even more important in magnetic ones. So is particle size. There is a fundamental size of a magnetic cluster below which it will exhibit only paramagnetic, not ferromagnetic, properties.

Another distinguishing feature of magnetic interactions is the nature of the role played by quantum mechanical phenomena. Exchange forces between the electrons, first within a single atom or ion, and then between nearest or next-nearest neighbor ion, or between itinerant electrons and those on fixed atoms in conductors, determine the short-range magnetic structure, which may be ferromagnetic, strongly or weakly ferrimagnetic, antiferromagnetic, or, of course non-magnetic or merely paramagnetic. In the former two cases, inclusion of the cooperative long-range magnetic forces determines the basic size (or domain) of the magnetic structure, which is also very shape-dependent. Magnetostrictive effects, particularly at surfaces, may also be a determining factor.

Finally, the dynamical properties of magnetism result from complex precessional interactions of the fixed and time-varying magnetic fields on the shape-dependent magnetization of the sample. If the material is a conductor, the electro-magnetic interactions with the mobile electrons must also be considered. And, of course, there are various relaxation mechanisms whereby the moving magnetization loses energy to the lattice. These differ substantially from the relaxation processes of moving charges with the lattice.

Our continually improving understanding of these physical properties has been essential in helping guide the development and inter-
pret the characteristics of experimental devices not only in the data
storage field we have chosen to describe, but also for a host of other
applications of magnetic materials ranging from permanent magnets
to transformer cores and nonreciprocal microwave circuit elements.

3.5 ELECTRICAL PROPERTIES OF MAGNETIC MATERIALS

Since a current generates a magnetic field and a changing magnetic
field generates an electromotive force, a number of important interactions exist between the magnetic and electrical properties of
matter. We have already mentioned the problem of eddy currents
in magnetic conductors, for example. These consequences of electro-
magnetic induction are well understood and subject to standard
engineering analysis — we shall not pursue them further. An almost
equally familiar topic is the Hall effect, whereby a current flowing
in a solid transverse to a magnetic field generates an EMF in a direction
perpendicular to both the current and the magnetic field. In semiconductors, the Hall effect is a research tool for investigating the
mobility and sign of the charge carriers; in ferromagnetic conductors
the phenomenon is somewhat more complicated. The Hall effect
also has technological applications and is one technique used for
the detection of the flux of magnetic bubbles, for instance. The
magneto-resistive effect, a different magneto-electric phenomenon,
is also a sensitive magnetic-field detector.

Two recent research fields: magnetic semiconductors and ferro-
electric-ferrimagnetic materials are also examples of investigations of
phenomena with potential technological interest. One must temper
this comment with the remark that it is likely that for technological
interest the material must be competitive in its primary function,
(e.g., magnetic), with "good" magnetic materials and then also have
its secondary properties (semiconductor or ferro-electric) be at
least "acceptably good" for a combined device to be useful.

3.6 SUMMARY

There are several important differences in the trends in magnetic in-
formation-storage technology and semiconductor technology. In
part, they are moving towards a common goal of integrated structures from different directions. Semiconductors approach integration as an evolution of discrete devices, whereas magnetics approaches
integration both from discrete devices (cores) and uniform thin-film
extensive storage media (tapes). There are differences also in the
variety of phenomena and materials of technolgical importance.

Technologically important magnetic phenomena, even for the relatively restricted application of data storage, occur in widely different type of magnetic materials, both insulators and conductors, and both magnetically hard and magnetically soft. On the other hand, a majority of the technologically important semiconductor devices can be optimally implemented in a single material, silicon. This generalization has been somewhat forced by considering only the electrical conduction of semiconductors, but including optical properties in the discussion of magnetic phenomena. For semiconductors, optical effects are sufficiently important as a subfield that they are treated separately in Chapter 5.

REFERENCES

1. A.H. Bobeck and H.E.D. Scovil, "Magnetic Bubbles," *Scientific American 224*, 78–90 (June 1971).

2. J.F. Dillon Jr., "Observation of Domains in Ferrimagnetic Garnets by Transmitted Light," *J. Appl. Phys. 29*, 1286–1291 (1958).

3. R.C. Sherwood, J.P. Remeika, and H.J. Williams, "Domain Behavior in Some Transparent Magnetic Oxides," *J. Appl. Phys. 30* 217–225 (1959).

4. C. Kooy and U. Enz, "Experimental and Theoretical Study of the Domain Configuration in Thin Layers of $BaFe_{12}O_{19}$," *Philips Research Reports 15*, 7–29 (1960).

5. H.J. Levinstein, S. Licht, R.W. Landorf, and S.L. Blank "Growth of High-Quality Garnet Thin Films from Supercooled Melts," *Appl. Phys. Lett. 19*, 486–488 (1971).

6. P. Chaudhari, J.J. Cuomo and R.J. Gambino, "Amorphous Magnetic Films for Bubble Domain Applications," *IBM J. Res. Develop. 17* 66–68 (1973).

7. C. Kittel and J.K. Galt, "Ferromagnetic Domain Theory," *Solid State Physics*, ed. Frederick Seitz and David Turnbull, (Academic Press, New York), Vol. 3, 437–564 (1956).

8. A. A. Thiele, "Theory of the Static Stability of Domains in Uniaxial Platelets", *J. Appl. Phys. 41*, 1139–1145 (1970). See also Ref. 4.

9. J.C. Slonczewski, "Dynamics of Magnetic Domain Walls," and B.E. Argyle, J.C. Slonczewski and A.F. Mayadas, "Domain Wall Motion in Rare-Earth Substituted Ga: YIG Epitaxial Films," *Proceedings 17th Conference on Magnetism and Magnetic Materials*, Chicago, Ill., Nov. 16-19, 1971.

    AIP Conference Proceedings #5, H.C. Wolfe, C.D. Graham Jr., and J.J. Rhyne Eds., American Institute of Physics, New York 1972, pp. 170–174 and 175–179.

10. Several papers in the 1973 International Magnetics Conference, Washington, D.C., April 24–27. The highest reported rate 1 Mbps was reported by R.C. LeCraw et al. "Localized Control of Magnetization in LPE Bubble Garnet Films, Paper 21.3.

11. J.B. Hagedorn, "Domain Wall Motion in Bubble Domain Materials," Proc. 17th Conf. on Mag. & Mag. Materials, Chicago, Ill., Nov. 16 & 19 (1971).

    AIP Conference Proceedings #5, H.C. Wolfe, C.D. Graham Jr., and J.J. Rhyne Eds., American Institute of Physics, New York 1972, pp. 72–90.

12. H.L. Hu, M. Hatzakis, E.A. Giess and T.S. Plaskett, "Shift Registers with Submicron Magnetic Bubbles in Epitaxial Garnet Films," 1973 International Magnetics Conference, Washington, D.C., April 24–27. paper 26.5.

13. P.I. Bonyhard and J.E. Geusic, "Magnetic Bubble Memory Chip Design", *ibid*, paper 21.7.

14. S. Chikazumi, *Physics of Magnetism* (John Wiley & Sons, New York, 1964). See also A.H. Agajanian, "Li-Mn Ferrites for High-Speed Computer Memory Applications," *IEEE Trans. Mag. 6*, 90–95 (1970).

15. A.H. Eschenfelder, "Promise of Magneto-Optic Storage Systems Compared to Conventional Magnetic Technology," *J. Appl. Phys. 41*. 1372–1376 (1970).

16. R.L. Comstock and P.H. Lissberger, "Magneto-Optic Properties of CrTe Films Prepared by Sequential Evaporation", *J. Appl. Phys. 41*, 1397–1398 (1970).

17. A.J. Kurtzig, R.L. Townsend, R. Wolfe, and J. Sosniak, "Reorientation and Curie Point Writing in Orthoferrites," *J. Appl. Phys. 42*, 1804–1805 (1971).

18. W.K. Unger, "Domain Configuration of Magnetic Holograms in Oriented MnBi Films," *Appl. Opt. 10*, 2788–2789 (1971).

19. J.A. Rajchman, "Promise of Optical Memories", *J. Appl. Phys. 41*, 1376–1383 (1970).

20. J.C. Suits, "Faraday and Kerr Effects in Magnetic Compounds," *IEEE Trans. on Magnetics, Mag. 8*, 95–105 (1972).

21. K.Y. Ahn and J.C. Suits, "Preparations and Properties of EuO Films," *IEEE Trans. Mag. 3* 453–455 (1967).

22. D. Chen, J.F. Ready and E. Bernal G., "MnBi Thin Films: Physical Properties and Memory Applications," *J. Appl. Phys. 39*, 3916–3927 (1968).

23. R.C. LeCraw, D.L. Wood, J.F. Dillon, Jr., and J.P. Remika, "The Optical Transparency of Yttrium Iron Garnet in the Near Infrared," *Appl. Phys. Lett. 7*, 27–28 (1965).

PROBLEMS

3.1 The theoretical basis for the statement of Eq. (3-3) involves a number of difficult and approximate relations. Using dimensional analysis, however, one can relate an energy kT_c to the exchange constant A and lattice constant a:

[aA] = [kT_c] or $aA = CkT_c$ where C is a dimensionless constant of the order of unity.

a. What does the above argument give as an estimate of A for iron? (Look up the relevant parameters.) For cobalt?

b. For a body centered cubic lattice material with a spin S = 1 (iron), a better theoretical approximation is C = 0.122. What is the corresponding value of A?

3.2 By how large a factor could the limit of Eq. (3-2) be reduced and still maintain an ideal detection signal to noise level of 100 if the noise is of purely thermal origin?

3.3 Following most workers in the respective fields, we use different units in Chapters 2 and 3. It is possible to put Eq. (3-19) and a combination of Eq.'s (2-4) and (2-5) in the same dimensional form as follows:

$$P_T = (Ne\ell)\ v_s/\mu\ \ \ = M_s\ v_s/\mu$$
$$\text{semiconducor} \quad \text{magnetic}$$

where $Ne\ell$ has the dimension of electrical polarization. In cgs units, energy density has the same form in terms of electric and magnetic fields ($E^2/8\Pi$ and $H^2/8\Pi$) for E in esu and H in emu or gauss. Hence, for comparison, change the semiconductor dimensions to esu (l esu = 300 volts/cm; e = 4.8 x 10^{-10} esu). Compare

a. [$Ne\ell$] for a FET with M_s and $4\Pi M_s$ for magnetic bubbles

b. v_s for a FET and for magnetic bubbles

c. μ for the two cases

d. Why is the figure of merit better for magnetic bubbles than for FET's?

3.4   Taking the quoted characteristics of MnBi Film,

a.   What is the optimum film thickness for detection of a laserpulse
      transmitted through crossed polarizers, with the film inserted be-
      tween the polarizers?

b.   What energy is required in a 100% polarized $\lambda = 0.63$ laserpulse
      for detection of a pulse with a signal-to-noise ratio (quantum
      limited) of 100?

c.   How does this compare with the energy required to heat a $1\,\mu m^2$
      area of the film $100°$ by a laser at the same frequency, assuming
      the parameters of problem 1.5 and no reflection losses?

Optics

In Chapters 1 through 3, developments emphasizing the increasing technological importance of surfaces and thin films were emphasized. The same morphological arguments are also shaping the new research field of "integrated optics" — i.e., optical circuits interconnected on or in a surface. Important additional ingredients influencing new advances in optical technology, however, are the availability of sources of highly coherent light, i.e. lasers, and the related emergence of holographic techniques of information processing. These latter ingredients are of the largely unplanned, revolutionary type that lead to unanticipated new applications and only accidentally improve existing ones. Indeed, we will see that maximized use of the *space coherence* property of lasers is incompatible with extreme miniaturization and miniaturized integrated optics. We also see that holography and most other types of optical data processing are most suited to performing parallel processing steps (image processing), and that there is a currently unresolved optoelectronic problem involved in optimizing the conversions between parallel optical data processing steps and serial electronic ones.

4.1 PARALLEL PROCESSING OF DATA OR MATERIALS

One great strength of optical technology is its ability to manipulate a large set of spatially compact data in a single operation. The data may be embodied by a high resolution transparency of an integrated circuit pattern, for example, and the operation is that of transferring this pattern to a semiconductor surface using a photoresist layer on the surface. Alternatively, the operation may be transmitting this information over moderate distances, perhaps for display purposes, as in a motion picture projector. Or the information may be processed, in a parallel mode, by optical techniques. The use of coherent (monochromatic, unidirectional) laser light and holographic techniques (Section 4.6) has revolutionized this type of optical data processing. To treat the subject in detail would require a mathematical and physical development differing substantially from that of the rest of this book — and one available in a number of recent texts and review articles.[1-3] Hence, we will restrict our development to a non-mathematical sketch of the basic principles of coherent data processing, with a few illustrative examples.

Consider Fig. 4-1, a system of two thin lenses separated by twice their identical focal lengths F. This is a complex lens system in which, for example, an object G located in the front focal plane of lens L_1 is imaged at P in the back focal plane of L_2. In our example, G is a grating with slot widths w and spacing d.

Coherent imaging of this grating may be described as follows:

1. The incident plane parallel monochromatic beam 0 of wave-length λ is diffracted by the grating into many beams according to the relation

   $$\sin \theta_m = m\lambda/d \qquad\qquad (4\text{-}1)$$

   where m is the diffraction order. In the figure, the zero, first and second order diffraction directions are shown.

2. The diffracted beams are brought to a common focus at P by the complex lens system. Interference among the orders re-constitutes the image.

3. The aperture of the complex lens itself, and other apertures, filters or other optical elements inserted in the optical path modify the image. Specifically, in Fig. 4-1, Lens L intercepts diffraction orders 0, 1 and 1 only. Hence L, acts as a *low pass optical filter*, rejecting all higher orders in θ. There is a loss of high resolution detail in the image at P since it is reconstituted from interference of the three lowest order beams only. The square edges of the grating are lost — only the basic periodicity in d is retained.

4. Between G and P, diffraction, beam shaping (the lenses) and interference effects result in various types of optical trans-formations. Near G and P these transformations are "out of focus" images. A particularly important transformation is shown in the plane F, where the filtered image of G is trans-formed into three points of light. Without developing the mathematics, this is a *Fourier transform* in space ($\times$, transverse to the light beam, replacing t and "spatial frequency" $\omega_x = 2\Pi/d$ replacing $\omega = 2\Pi f$). In turn, the image at P is the Fourier transform of the three coherent point sources at F.

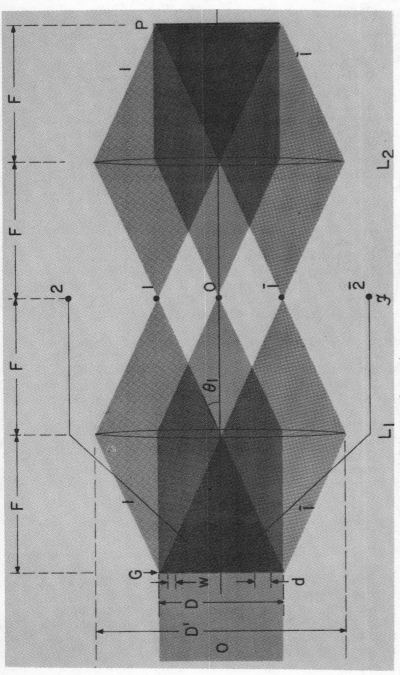

Figure 4-1. Fourier Transform and Filtering Operations

An object G (a grating) in the front focal plane of lens L_1 is Fourier transformed to the dot pattern $\cdot\cdot 2, 1, 0, 1, \overline{2}\cdot\cdot$, in the back focal plane of L_1. This transform is low-pass filtered by the finite aperature of the lens to $1, 0, \overline{1}$ which is again Fourier transformed by L_2 to a degraded reproduction of the grating in plane P. All object-lens & lens-transform distances are F, the focal length of each lens. Reproduced from "Laser Applications," with permission of Artech House.

The optical filtering and Fourier transform steps 3 and 4 above are examples of coherent optical data processing performed in parallel on all elements of the transmitted image. A more complicated data procession step is that of image deblurring. We are familiar with the fact that our own out-of-focus negatives cannot be restored simply by adjusting the focus of the projector — however, it is clear that it is some deficiency in the recording process on photographic film that causes the difficulty: the defocussed images in Fig. 4-1 and ultimately come to a correct focus at P. It is by no means obvious, but it is plausible, that more sophisticated optical techniques can indeed deblur out-of-focus optical images or images blurred by motion, and in fact coherent optical data processing can accomplish these results even if the original image was recorded in "ordinary" non-coherent light.[3]

Our illustrations all involve image processing, and we can add analyzing the images — comparing the data in the image with reference data in either the Fourier transform or reference plane. Pattern recognition and classification would be an example. Other examples exist in which high density information — such as that obtained from side-looking microwave radar — are processed optically. In all cases, successful applications involve performing simple geometric diffraction and interference operations on a mass of optical data in a plane. (We note that the special place of planes in these examples corresponds to the importance of surfaces in our earlier chapters.) In those cases where all operations are sequential in space, and time-invariant, (i.e., fixed filters), they proceed with the speed of light through the optical system, and since many bits are operated on in parallel in each step, the information throughput is tremendous. This form of optical data processing has therefore become well established. Its time-averaged optical throughput is apt to be determined by the rate of generating the data in the first place (perhaps by the mechanical motion of photographic films). If changeable optical filters are also incorporated in the processing more information can be extracted from the original data set with a comparable time-averaged optical throughput.

4.2 COHERENCE PROPERTIES OF LASERS[4]

The important coherence properties of laser oscillators utilized in coherent data processing are the directionality and monochromaticity of the emitted light. These two properties are known, respectively, as space coherence and time coherence, and measured quantitatively as radiance and spectral radiance. The ability of mode-locked lasers to generate trains of very short pulses is also a special form of time coherence.

The radiance of any light source is defined as the optical power per unit solid angle intercepted by a unit surface area

$$R = P/A\delta\Omega \tag{4-2}$$

For a diffraction limited laser source, the solid angle is determined by the diffraction spread of the aperture area A of the laser mirrors

$$\delta\Omega \cong \lambda^2/A \tag{4-3}$$

hence

$$R_L \cong P/\lambda^2 \tag{4-4}$$

It is appropriate to compare this radiance with that of an incoherent light source radiating out from a bounding surface S:

$$R_i = P/CS \tag{4-5}$$

where $C = 4\pi$ for isotropic radiation or 2π for radiation following Lambert's law. If the sources have the same power output and bounding surface S — i.e., the same ability to dissipate heat, assuming equal efficiencies of light generation — the brightness ratio of the two sources is

$$R_L/R_i \cong CS/\lambda^2. \tag{4-6}$$

This is a factor of 10^9 for a typical Nd YAG laser with $S = 1\text{cm}^2$ and $\lambda = 1\mu\text{m}$. The spectral radiance of a light source is its radiance divided by its bandwidth, which is typically orders of magnitude narrower for a laser than a non-laser source. Hence the spectral radiance advantage of lasers is even greater than their radiance advantage. Our discussion of applications for these coherence advantages of lasers will range beyond purely opto-electronic and optical data processing ones in order to put in perspective their promise in these latter fields.

4.3 ELECTRO-OPTIC PHENOMENA[5,6]

The interfaces between optical and non-optical phenomena — electrical, magnetic, acoustic — are active areas of current investigation since it is often necessary either to control optical energy non-optically or to change from one form of energy flow to another. Classical examples are photodetection and cathodoluminescence of phosphors. Newer ones are electro-magneto- and acousto-optics and p-n junction electroluminescence. The control of light by light is also a branch of opto-electronics including such diverse recent subjects as nonlinear optics and the amorphous-crystalline phase changes in thin films brought about by intense pulses of optical energy.

In the above list the electrical energy conversion examples are strong effects, often manifest in thin films or surface layers. At frequencies above or near the band gap of the material in question, optical energy can be converted to electrical energy with high quantum efficiency and in very short distances, distances shorter than the wavelength of light. Photography and semiconductor photodetection are familiar examples. In cathodoluminescence and p-n junction electroluminescence the inverse energy conversion is also efficient, and the penetration depths and diffusion lengths of the charge carriers often determine even shorter interaction distances. On the other hand the optical energy control phenomena are weaker effects, and very much weaker if the material is essentially transparent to the light being controlled. There is thus a wide-open competition as to which of these weak effects, electromagnet or acousto-optic, will prove the more useful in devices. Indeed, there is a question whether any of them will be useful enough to extend the applications of laser technology to to certain areas where high-speed spatially compact control of the radiation is an important consideration.

a.   Electro-optics

In Chapter 3 we illustrated some magneto-optic magnitudes. Here we will consider two electro-optic effects for comparison, deferring planar integrated optics, however, to Section 4-4. We consider first the linear electro-optic effect, manifest in certain transparent dielectric materials of appropriate symmetry, in which an applied electric field changes the birefringence Δn of the material. The effect may be either longitudinal, with the light traveling in the direction of the applied field (in which case transparent electrodes are used) or transverse, with the light direction perpendicular to that of the electric field. The governing equation is [5]

$$\Delta n = n^3 r E / 2 \qquad\qquad (4\text{-}7)$$

defining the electro-optic coefficient r (actually a tensor; we simplify to one component only). Consider a cube of thickness ℓ of initially isotropic material. Upon application of a voltage V across two faces the material becomes anisotropic. Light polarized at 45° to two principal axes then experiences a relative retardation $\Delta n \ell$ after passing through the crystal (Fig. 4-2). When this retardation is π, the polarization is rotated 90° after passing through the crystal, and the intensity of the light transmitted by an analyzer oriented to pass the initial polarization vanishes. The so-defined half wave voltage V_π is given by

$$\Delta n\ell = \lambda/2 \qquad\qquad\qquad\qquad\qquad\qquad (4\text{-}8)$$

$$V_\pi = E\ell = \lambda/n^3 r \qquad\qquad\qquad\qquad\qquad (4\text{-}9)$$

It is seldom less than 1,000 volts in materials of good optical quality.

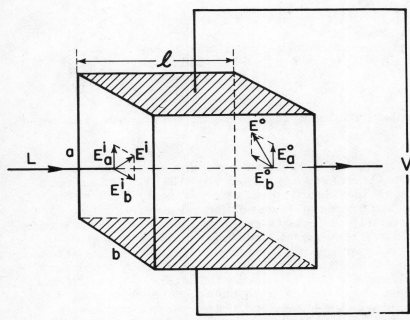

Figure 4-2.   Electro-Optic Modulation
Light plane polarized in the direction E^i at 45° to the
principle optic axes a and b is resolved into the components
E_a^i and E_b^i on entering on electro-optic crystal. A voltage
V applied to electrodes, here shown as appropriate for the
transverse electro-optic effect, generates a refractive index difference $n_b - n_a = \Delta n$. The retardation of E_b^o for the
light exiting the crystal is 180°, as shown, if $\Delta n\ell = \lambda/2$,
and the exiting light polarization is rotated 90°.

Eq. (4-6) holds also for materials that are not optically isotropic, and
indeed all materials with reasonably low values of V_π are ferroelectric,
and hence anistropic, either at their operating temperature or at
some lower temperature. For such materials very general relations
have been derived relating V_π to material parameters. There seems to
be little reason to expect dramatic decreases in this quantity in the
foreseeable future.

Electro-optic light modulators are frequently used in the transverse mode. Device analyses similar in principle to those used in Chapter 2 and 3 lead to a power per unit band width — i.e., a power-time constant product[7]

$$P_T = C\lambda K V_\pi^2 \qquad (4-10)$$

where K is the dielectric constant of the material and C is independent of the material. Unfortunately, low V_π is associated with high K. In reference 7 the best modulator listed, using $LiNbo_3$ for which $KV_\pi^2 \approx 3 \times 10^7$ volts^2 at $\lambda = 0.63\,\mu m$, had a value

$$P_T \approx 1 \text{ nanojoule,} \qquad (4-11)$$

a value substantially larger than for most of the phenomena quoted in Chapters 2 and 3.

For many purposes a more attractive electro-optic phenomenon might be the birefringence associated with bistably switching a ferro-electric rather than electro-optically modulating it. This is not as mature a field for analysis as that of linear electro-optic effects for two reasons: (1) Ferroelectric switching is not as well controlled a phenomenon as ferromagnetic switching and (2) only rarely is longitudinal birefringence associated with 180° ferroelectric switching (the most useful geometry for display and memory applications). A recent advance in both categories is the development of ferroelectric ceramics. These are lead-lanthanum-zirconium tantalate materials with a variety of birefringence and hysteresis loop properties, depending on chemical compositions, size of ceramic grains, and state of mechanical strain of the material.[8] Some single crystal boracite materials also exhibit birefrigence on 180° ferroelectric switching.[9,10] For a square loop material, the switching energy is the electrical analog of the magnetic case Eq. (3-22), i.e.,

$$E = 2E_C P_S \qquad (4-12)$$

where P_S is the saturation polarization and E_C the coercive field. The range of these parameters in materials with desired optical properties is less known than for magnetic materials. For the boracite $Fe_3B_7O_{13}I$, with a switchable birefringence of $\pm.002$ at room temperature, the polarization may be deduced to be about 3×10^3 esu and the coercive field (not necessarily square loop) in the range of 5 to 20 kilovolts per cm. The corresponding P_T product is

$$P_T = E \approx 2 \times 10^5 \text{ ergs/cm}^3 = 2.10^{-2} \text{ picojoules/}\mu m^3 \qquad (4-13)$$

If one seeks to use the 100% modulation of Eq. (4-9) the value $\Delta n =$ 2x.002, with $\lambda = 0.5\,\mu m$ gives a required thickness $\ell = 60\,\mu m$, or a $P\tau$ product of 4.3 nanojoules for a $60\,\mu m$ cube. Similar refractive index changes and similar switching energies are associated with ferroelectric ceramics.[8, 11] Moreover, the switching time constants in both cases are in the microsecond or longer category. Hence, these characteristics are promising for display purposes where the relatively coarse resolution and long time constants are adequate.

Related materials are known with larger birefringence, allowing higher resolution. However still less is known about their switching characteristics. For memory rather than display purposes it is also satisfactory to switch a phase shift φ of much less than π radians, utilizing a readout between crossed polarizers proportional to $\sin^2 \varphi$. In the example chosen, for $\ell = 4\,\mu m$, this would be 4.4% of the maximum signal, with $P\tau$ product of 1.3 picojoules.

The often ill-defined hysteresis loops of these materials sometimes lead to device designs incorporating sandwiches of ferroelectric and photoconductive materials, where the region to be switched is defined by the low resistance of an illuminated spot on the photoconductor.[12] In this case more restrictive photoconductor time constants, and power consumption tend to dominate the device.

b. Mostly Acousto-optic and Other Electro-optic Phenomena

Acousto-optic phenomena are quite competitive with electro-optic ones for the modulation and deflection of light, but lack the memory potential of electro-optic phenomena. The passage of a sound wave through a transparent material sets up a moving diffraction grating resulting from periodic changes in the refractive index at peaks and troughs of the sound wave.[5, 13] All transparent material — glasses, crystals of all symmetries — exhibit this property to a greater or lesser extent. Hence the materials selection possibilities are much less restrictive than for electro-optic materials.

It is perhaps useful to illustrate the magnitude of acousto-optic phenomena by some of the properties of acousto-optic deflection illustrated in Fig. 4-3. This is one component of the holographic storage system we discuss in Section 4.6, and indeed a component which cannot be miniaturized since it must operate on an optical beam a millimeter or more in diameter.

A complete analysis must interrelate the acoustic and optical wavelengths Λ and λ, the incident angle φ of the acoustic beam, the deflection angle θ of the diffracted light beam, and the diffraction

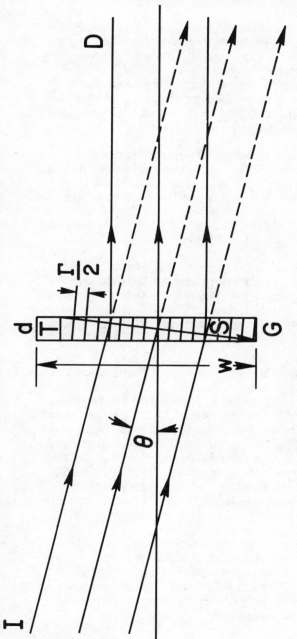

Figure 4-3   Acousto-Optic Deflector
An incident monochromatic collimated light beam I is diffracted by a moving acoustic grating G, generated by a sound beam S launched by a piezo-electric transducer T. The grating spacing $\Lambda/2$, wavelength λ and diffraction angle θ are related by Eq. (4-14), and the sound beam bisects the angle between I and the diffracted beam direction D. The acoustic and optical apertures are d and w.

angular spreads $\delta\varphi$ and $\delta\theta$ of the acoustic and optical beam. The pertinent relations are

$$2 \sin\left(\frac{\theta}{2}\right) = \lambda/\Lambda = \lambda\, f/v \tag{4-14}$$

$$\varphi = \theta/2 \tag{4-15}$$

$$\delta\theta \approx \lambda/w \tag{4-16}$$

and

$$\delta\varphi \approx \Lambda/d \tag{4-17}$$

where d and w are the thickness and width, i.e., the acoustic and optic apertures of the deflector, and v is the acoustic velocity. It is experimentally convenient to tune the acoustic frequency f, which correspondingly varies Λ since $\Lambda f = v$ = constant. Varying Λ then changes θ accordingly to Eq. (4-14), but Eq. (4-15) is a restriction since it states that one must simultaneously change φ. Sometimes this is done by making T in Fig. 4-3 a phased array transducer[14]. Alternatively, d is made small enough that $\delta\varphi$ becomes comparable to φ and Eq. (4-17) replaces Eq. (4-15) as the supplementary condition to Eq. (4-14). Finally, approximating $\sin\theta/2$ by $\theta/2$, the deflection resolution, i.e., number of resolved spots N, is given by

$$N = \frac{\Delta\theta}{\delta\theta} = \left(\frac{\lambda\Delta f}{v}\right)\left(\frac{w}{\lambda}\right) = \tau\Delta f \tag{4-18}$$

where τ and Δf are the acoustic transit time and bandwidths. In a deflector designed according to the above prescription, it required something over one watt of continuous RF power, tuneable over a 170 MHz bandwidth to achieve a resolution of 200 spots of Argon laser light ($\lambda = 5145\text{Å}$) transmitted through the long dimension of a 5mm x 5mm x 10mm sample of $PbMo_4$, a particularly efficient acousto-optic material.[14] The center modulation frequency was 288 MHz, and the achieved diffraction efficiency 50%. The acoustic velocity of 4×10^5 cm/sec gives a value of 1.2 μs for τ. From Eq. (4-17) the product $1.2 \times 10^{-6} \times 170 \times 10^6$ is the quoted resolution of 200 spots. Thus two such deflectors in series, one for x and one for y deflection, could deflect 4×10^4 resolution elements at a time constant of 1.2×10^{-6} seconds for 2 watts of input power. A figure of merit might be

$$P\tau/N = 2 \times 1.2 \times 10^{-6}/4 \times 10^4 = 6 \times 10^{-9} \text{ joules} \tag{4-19}$$

i.e., 6 nanojoules per bit, comparable to electro-optic modulation magnitudes.

Finally, we should mention the controlled scattering of light in liquid crystals[15] (and in one mode of operation of ferroelectric ceramics[8]), the glass-to-crystal and metal-to-insulator phase changes associated with local heating[16] , and magneto-optic readout of magnetic bubbles. The liquid crystal phenomena are slow (milliseconds) but suitable for displays. The thermally induced phase changes have energy requirements similar to the magneto-thermal example analysed in Chapter 3. Magneto-optic phenomena and magnetic bubble propagation are also discussed in Chapter 3.

4.4   PLANAR INTEGRATED OPTICS

Before examining optical data processing applications it is necessary to introduce another technology which is in a still earlier state of development than the three topics; lasers, coherent optics, and optoelectronics; already discussed. It is in fact the miniaturization and integration of these phenomena into the single technology of planar integrated optics. The following definition is useful for our purposes:

"Integrated optics is a planar technology wherein optical information either channeled within a plane or traveling transverse to the plane is processed by other information, optical or non-optical, channeled within the plane."

This breadth of definition, and the infancy of the subject, suggests that qualitative analysis is more useful for our purposes than quantitative analysis. The following points are important:

1.   Appropriate refractive index variations at the planar surfaces can keep optical energy channeled within the plane. Indeed, refractive index tailoring within the plane can further channel the optical paths within the plane.

2.   Similar boundary conditions can also channel acoustical energy within the plane and within specific paths in the plane.

These two   points give the well appreciated result that

3.   Optoelectronic phenomena channeled within a plane can be better miniaturized and consume less power than bulk optoelectronic devices, (by perhaps a factor of five for a thin film counterpart of the example of Eq. (4-1))[17] . This is because optical (and acoustic, if this is the optoelectronic phenomenon under consideration) diffraction losses and path spreading are minimized.

If one is concerned with processing optical information traveling transverse to the plane, another consideration is important.

4. Microminiaturized electronic information can travel within the plane without spreading. Therefore, high resolution transformations to and from electronic information traveling within the plane and optical information traveling transverse to the plane are possible. Examples are the readout of optical images by charge transfer devices (Chapter 2) and the read in of optical images by magnetic bubbles. In both cases shift registers within the plane move the electronic data to and from regions within the optical image.

Subsequent sections of this chapter relate the optical technologies discussed so far to data processing.

4.5 PARALLEL INFORMATION TRANSMISSION BY COHERENT LIGHT

In contact printing the coherence properties of lasers are not useful; what counts is adequate power spread uniformly over the surface. Consider, however, the projection printing, transmission or display of an optical pattern. Here, if the pattern is of low resolution, and the area to be illuminated small, there is an advantage to using lasers. The directionality allows one to use smaller lenses, or to dispense with them entirely in extreme cases. On the other hand, if there is high spatial frequency detail in the image to be transmitted, its diffraction spread will still require large lenses and the laser advantage is diminished.

Optimization of tradeoffs for image transmission, using lasers, is a complicated subject with considerable current activity, both theoretical and experimental. It is, of course, influenced by the optical system under consideration. One of the more promising ones is the "self-foc" optical fiber, a material with a parabolic decrease in refractive index from the center of the fiber.[18] Among its many interesting properties, such a fiber, which can collect light most efficiently from a coherent laser source with small numerical aperture optics, refocuses periodically along its length an image formed at its entrance face. As with all periodic optical transmission systems however, (for instance, equally spaced lenses), the quality of the image degrades with distance. I.e., the modes of the transmission system into which the image can be decomposed have different attenuation constants and also are intermixed by imperfections in the transmission system.[19] If the overall attenuation is more severe than the degradation, laser image amplifiers can provide the necessary gain.[20]

Advances in laser and optical technology also make possible two other forms of parallel information transmission, plus a serial form discussed in Section 4.8. One form of image transmission is to transmit the image over a bundle of optical fibers rather than a self-foc fiber. This is a well-known technique for short distances. However, the attenuation of optical fibers has now been made so low (less than 20 dB per kilometer[21]) that this technique, using repeaters and amplifiers, in principle could be extended to long distances. More practically, the individual, optically isolated fibers can be used for separate information streams unrelated to direct image transmission.

Instead of using the space coherence features of lasers, as in image transmission, analogy with conventional lower frequency information transmission suggests making use of the time coherence — i.e., the narrow bandwidth in combination with the directionality of the beam. In this approach one uses only the lowest order mode of the transmission system — the mode with the least attenuation — and frequency multiplexes the tremendous available optical bandwidth to send many streams of data in parallel over the same transmission line. The optical bandwidth between $\lambda \pm 0.5 \, \mu$m and 1μm is 10,000 cm^{-1}, or 3×10^{14} Hz. Allowing a generous 30 KHz per two-way voice channel, this bandwidth has the potential of 10 billion simultaneous voice conversations over a single spatial channel. Even at a video bandwidth, 100 million video-phone conversations would be possible. However, at present, the needs of data transmission are only a fraction of non-data needs. Clearly there is no present necessity to exploit all this bandwidth. A typical proposed frequency multiplexed system indeed utilizes only a single laser (YAG, λ = 1.1μm) providing 12 carriers, each with a 10^9 Hz optical bandwidth.[22] The rate of commercial acceptance of optical information transmission is likely to be at least as closely related to the cost element as to the performance element of achieving improved cost/performance compared to present technology.

4.6 HOLOGRAPHIC IMAGE STORAGE AND RETRIEVAL

Consider next the intermediate storage of an image. Here holographic laser techniques provide considerable versatility which has yet to be exploited fully, primarily because the associated technical problems are severe. Holography is a recent but well developed science described in a number of texts.[1-3, 23] Laser holographic storage is essentially the storage of an interference pattern between time coherent laser light scattered or transmitted by an object and a space-and-time coherent fraction of the same laser light used as a reference beam. A lensless way of making holograms and reconstructing images from them is illustrated in Fig. 4-4. The interference pattern may

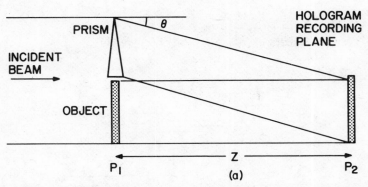

Figure 4-4A. Wedge technique for producing a two-beam hologram.

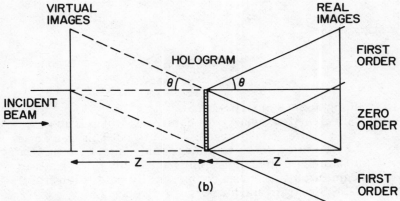

Figure 4-4B. The reconstruction process.
High quality reconstructions occur in the first order
diffracted waves. By permission from William V.
Smith, "Laser Applications," Artech House, Inc.,
Dedham, Mass. (1970).

be stored either in two dimensions, as in a photographic film, or in
three dimensions, as refractive index variations throughout a more
or less extended volume. In either case, illumination of the stored
interference pattern by another reference beam, simply related to
the initial reference beam, reproduces the original object as a real or
virtual three dimensional image in space. Of course, so storing and
reproducing two dimensional images as a special case of three dimensional image storage has its own class of potential applications. A
possible data storage embodiment, using an optical system closely
related to that of Fig. 4-1, is illustrated in Fig. 4-5.

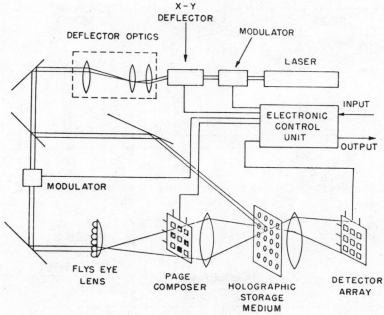

Figure 4-5. Holographic Memory System.
        Data are entered via a page composer, which is an array
        of x-y addressed light valves or shutters. This transforms
        the data bits into a two dimensional digital pattern. Data
        are stored on the holographic medium by passing a laser
        beam through the page composer. By permission from
        IEEE Spectrum and authors of reference 24.

a. Two Dimensionsional Holographic Data Storage

In Fig. 4-5 a light deflector can switch a laser beam to address any
one of, say, 10^5 small holograms (each about 1mm in diameter)
arranged systematically on a plane.[24] This hologram storage plane
can be the front focal plane of a lens as in Fig. 4-1, in which case the
far field pattern of *each individual hologram* covers *a single area* with
unit magnification. (Note that sliding the grating, a special hologram,
up and down in Fig. 4-1 does not change the location of the dots in
plane F.) In Fig. 4-5 the planes are so chosen that demagnification
occurs between the image plane (the page composer) and the hologram plane.

In the detector array plane there is a regular array of, say, 10^5 photodetectors. If each hologram has been made by illuminating an equivalent array of optoelectronically controlled holes in a mask in the page

composer, some open and some closed to represent the data, the corresponding pattern of light and dark areas will fall on the photodetectors which then can read a 10^5 bit "page" of data in parallel. Fig. 4-6 shows the transformation between a magnetic Curie-point hologram and a detector matrix.

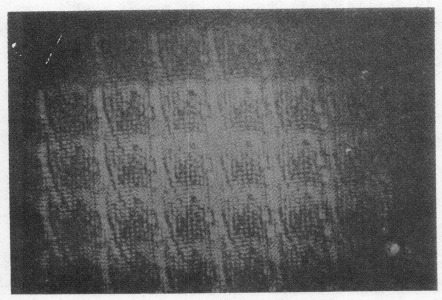

Figure 4-6.   Magnetic Curie-point Hologram written on a MnBi thin film.[25]
(A)   Original hologram

There are four apparent strengths to this form of data storage:

1.   The data can be stored redundantly in the hologram: i.e., a scratch in the hologram only degrades the bit image uniformly rather than eliminating specific bits.

2.   Pages can be addressed electronically without mechanical motion by the light beam deflection.

3.   The data from each page can be read rapidly in parallel and

4.   The system is insensitive to small lateral motions of the holograms.

Of the strengths (1) is somewhat over-rated. (There are more efficient ways of incorporating data redundancy) and (3) is not unique:

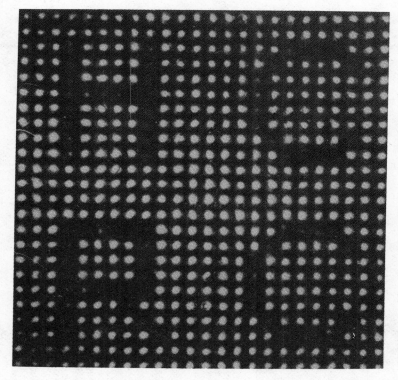

Figure 4-6. Magnetic Curie-point Hologram written on a MnBi
thin film. (cont.)
(B)   Reconstructed image consisting of 24-24 bits. By
permission from Applied Optics.

one can also incorporate parallel reading in other data storage systems. Item (4) can be helpful but involves tradeoffs in sensitivity
to angular displacement. Item (2) is potentially quite important,
but quantitatively requires improvement in deflection technology to
be a determining factor.

Unfortunately, the previous list of strengths is accompanied by some
weaknesses:

5.   The data storage is slightly less dense than with purely digital
      arrays.

6.   In the present and near future state-of-the-art, read-only mem-
      ories are possible, but read-write memories require substantial
      further technological advances.

Item (5) above is not serious; however item (6) is, as it severely limits the breadth of applications. While some serious problems exist with the recording medium, the most serious one is in the writing[11, 26], — i.e., in modulating the transparency of the holes in the mask sufficiently rapidly and with low power dissipation. We will consider the problem further in the next section.

As a related subject, holograms of photographic masks may be used in photo-resist processing of integrated circuits. Here lasers are essential, in contrast to the situation in contact printing where they were not useful. Items (1) and (4) in the above "strengths" list are important. There are penalties too, requiring careful examination, which, however, we will not discuss.

b. Holographic Storage of Three Dimensional Images

We have mentioned the 3-D image features of holographic storage. This, of course, conjures up exciting visions of 3-D movies, home television, etc. Some of these visions probably are in our future, but the technological and, in some cases, psychological obstacles are severe. (3-D on a reduced size scale, as in home TV, is said to convey the unrealistic impression of a marionette show). The information content of 3-D TV is too large for standard transmission, and large screen laser movies await the development of higher power, more efficient lasers, in the visible, preferably with a range of color capabilities. On the other hand, a holographic record of a three dimensional data set can instantaneously record a large volume of object space without loss of resolution either from aberrations or depth of focus. This record can subsequently be examined at leisure.

c. Data Storage in Three Dimensional Holograms

Not only can 3-D images be stored in 2-D holograms but also, as mentioned in Chapter 1, 2-D images can be stored in 3-D holograms.

In essence, volume holographic storage results from transforming the spatial localization of a data point in the focal plane of a lens to the ray-direction localization of a light beam on the other side of the lens. A record of this ray direction is then made by means of the interference fringes of the intersection of the data-point light beam with a reference light beam of the same frequency but a different direction. See Fig. 4-7, which also shows that the fringe planes bisect the angle θ between the directions of propagation of the two coherent interfering wave trains. They occur at a spacing

$$d = \left(\frac{\lambda}{2}\right) \cos\left(\frac{\theta}{2}\right) \tag{4-20}$$

where θ is the angle between the ray directions.

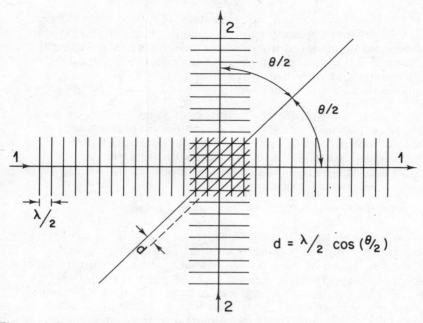

Figure 4-7. Three Dimensional Holographic Recording

      (A) Volume interference grating. Diagonal fringes of separation d are formed in a photographic emulsion at the intersection of two orthogonal coherent light beams of wavelengths λ.

The interference fringes are recorded by some local nonlinear detection process — for instance, one proportional to the time-averaged intensity of the light — i.e., a photographic or photochromic record.

Now, it is possible to make use of the periodic variation in absorption of light by the recorded fringes to reconstruct (i.e., read) the original data point. However, a better procedure is to convert this absorption variation into a refractive index variation. This forms a dielectric grating. One way of doing this is to bleach the photographic emulsion. The variation in density resulting from removing the silver grains results in a refractive index variation. Alternatively, a form of photochromic recording, operating in a nearly transparent window of the material and utilizing a reversible fixing process is currently under investigation.[27]

Fig. 4-7A shows a dielectric grating of spacing d formed by the intersection of two beams, 1 and 2, wavelength λ. Assume first that this is a bleached photographic emulsion with no change in d accompanying the bleaching. Then if this grating is again illuminated by beam 1,

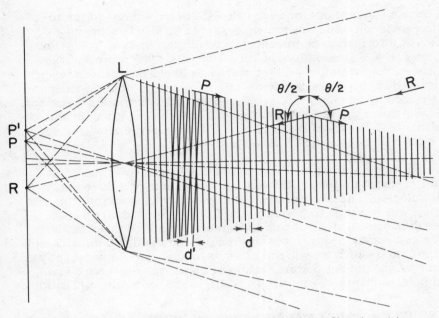

Figure 4-7. Three Dimensional Holographic Recording (cont.)

(B) Hologram formation and reconstruction. Coherent point sources P and P′, and reference point R are transformed by lens L to ray directions P, P′ and R. The interference fringes of P with R (spacing d, intersection angle θ) and P′ with R (spacing d′) are also shown.

part of this beam will be scattered in direction 2. The law of coherent scattering is the same as that of interference, Eq. (4-20). Reference to Fig. 4-7B shows that, if beams from P (traveling to the right) and R (traveling to the left) interfere to form a grating, illumination of the grating by a beam from point R will form a back scattered point image at P, thus "reading" point P as recorded in the emulsion. Many pages of data can be recorded in the same volume by rotating the recording medium (and consequently the recorded fringes) some angle φ after the first image plane is recorded. In this new position, if φ is large enough, the reconstruction beam R will no longer form an image in the data plane. In the new position, however, new fringes can be recorded and the corresponding images reconstructed. The ultimate limit on storage density (number of pages that can be stored time resolution elements in each page) is determined by the aperture of the system and the resolution of the gratings which set a lower limit on φ.

With certain assumptions, one can calculate that a volume of photo-sensitive material, using this principle, should be able to store an amount of information approaching its resolution limit of V/λ^3. For $\lambda = 1\mu m$ and $V = 1cm^3$, this would be 10^{12} bits! The prospect, there-fore, has excited technological interest. It is likely that various fac-tors ignored in this estimate — cross talk arising from nonlinearities in the recording medium, spatial noise in the refractive index variations, etc. — will lower this density appreciably; nonetheless, it still might be substantial. How useful would such a storage medium be if, say, 10^{10} bits could be stored in this fashion?

At present there is no known way to selectively erase portions of in-formation stored uniformly throughout the volume of a three dimen-sional hologram, and one can advance physical arguments that this situation will continue to prevail in the future. (Individual sheets of a three dimensional stack of thin holograms perhaps can be selectively written and erased in situ,[28] but this is a different and still more compli-cated situation which we will not attempt to analyze). Consequently it seems safe to predict that utilization of homogeneous three dimen-sional holographic memories will be restricted to read-only applications.

4.7 SERIAL — PARALLEL DATA CONVERSION

A serious problem impeding more widespread utilization of parallel optical data processing is establishing a practical transformation be-tween the serial electrical data format of conventional computers and the parallel format of optics. The need here is for fast, thoroughly miniaturized and integrated low power electro-optic switches and storage elements. Consider, for example, the conversion problem of matching a serial data flow rate F to a parallel data flow rate R of pages of m bits each:

$$F = mR \qquad\qquad (4\text{-}21)$$

The means that in the interface or "page composer", the m bits must be addressed at the high serial rate F although, if they can store the addressing information, they need respond only at slower rate R. The interesting range of F for logic devices is 10^8 to 10^{10} sec^{-1}, which, for the data set of $m = 10^5$, we have been considering gives a range of R from 10^3 to 10^5 sec^{-1}. For display applications (i.e., at the end of the data processing line) these ranges can be relaxed somewhat. The result is that liquid crystal time constants are suitable for dis-play but probably not for logic even if the slow rate R is the deter-mining factor. Magnetic bubbles can respond at the display rate R, and higher. At present their magneto-optical efficiency however is marginal at best. The miniaturized semiconductor modulator which we will discuss in the next section has adequate time constants, but one undesirably long dimension (1 mm) which would seem to preclude its use in the integrated geometrics involved. Row-at-a-time organized ferroelectric ceramic page composers can operate at a 10μ sec per row switching rate.[11]

4.8 SERIAL OPTICAL PROCESSING, DATA TRANSMISSION, AND MINIATURIZATION

In contrast to parallel processing, where spatially complicated material patterns are not easily changed rapidly, serial processing can be more individually tailored to changing events. The data streams in conventional digital computers require frequent redirections in time, and hence are primarily serial in nature. Are lasers suitable for serial operations?

Optical radar[4] is one practical type of serial optical data processing. Eq. (4-3), interpreted to minimize $\delta\Omega$, shows the angular precision possible with moderate size optical antennas. At $\lambda = 1\mu m$ and A = $1cm^2$ this is 20 seconds of arc! Atmospheric conditions degrade this performance, but for short ranges, or high altitudes, or good weather, it is very useful. Similarly, narrow angular optical beams are useful for on earth surveying and communications in space.

Let us now consider the properties of miniaturized lasers and integrated optics. Referring to Eq. (4-6), we see that miniaturizing a laser decreases its brightness advantage compared to an incoherent light source. Thus small lasers, either in integrated optic structures, or used to read individual memory bits, necessarily must sacrifice some of the laser's unique characteristics. Nevertheless, a substantial, and generally adequate advantage remains compared to incoherent light sources. For example, arrays of miniaturized GaAs injection lasers [29] have junction areas $13\mu m$, by $400\mu m$, with $\lambda = 0.9\mu m$. Using Eq. (4-6) with Lambert's law value of $C = 2\pi$, these lasers; when diffraction limited, are still 40,000 times brighter than incoherent diodes of the same area and power output. In the limit of a one dimensional optical fiber laser Eq. (4-6) becomes

$$R_L/R_i \cong C\ell/\lambda \qquad\qquad (4-22)$$

where ℓ is the length of the fiber. In high gain lasers values of ℓ as small as 10λ has been achieved (not in fiber configurations yet). Even such a short fiber laser would be 60 times as bright as the equivalent volume incoherent light source. (On the other hand, as already noted, a more typical solid state laser, such as Nd YAG, is brighter than the equivalent incoherent light source by the much more impressive figure of 10^9 , a factor fully utilized in materials processing, radar, communications and surveying applications). Of course, some applications of small lasers may also use their time coherence (their monochromaticity). In these cases the comparison is more favorable for the laser.

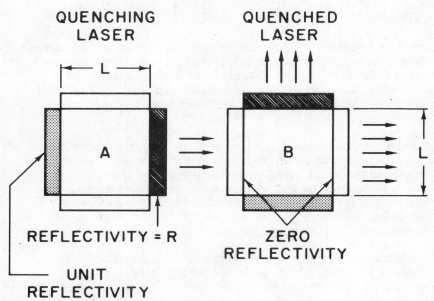

Figure 4-8.   Laser Inverter Circuit
Beam from laser A (horizontal) quenches beam from laser
B (vertical). Reproduced from Lasher and Fowler[30] by
permission of the IBM Journal of Research and Development.

Serial magneto-optic data storage, a promising application, was treated
in Chapter 3. The GaAs laser arrays discussed above are suitable for
this application and similar lasers are the basis of part of our following discussion of serial optical logic operations. We will wish to compare electrical semiconductor technology, treated in Chapter 2, with
optical semiconductor technology. The laser-quenched-laser inverter
circuit of Fig. 4-8 illustrates the principles and magnitudes involved.[30]
The equilibrium population inversion of Laser A is perturbed when
the saturation parameter

$$2I_B \sigma \tau \rightarrow 1 \qquad\qquad\qquad (4\text{-}23)$$

where I_B is the flux in photons/sec cm^2 from laser A incident on

laser B and σ is the cross section for the laser radiation.[31] If the per-
turbation is great enough, laser B is quenched and ceases to oscillate.
Combinations of these circuits with optical feedback loops consti-
tute bistable optical flip-flops that can be used to perform logic operations. Similar devices including saturable optical absorbers in the
circuits obey a similar equation.[32]

The quenching power P and figure of merit $P\tau$ corresponding to Eq.
(4-23) are

$$P = h\nu I_B A = h\nu A/2\sigma\tau \tag{4-24}$$

$$P\tau = h\nu A/2\sigma \tag{4-25}$$

where A is the cross sectional area of the laser. We see that for laser
logic, $P\tau$ is proportional to ν, and hence a tradeoff exists between miniaturization (decreasing λ) and minimizing $P\tau$ (decreasing ν).

There is no simple way to determine a *practical* upper bound on σ, and
indeed, for gases with allowed dipole transitions (the sodium D lines,
for example), σ is about 5×10^{-12} cm^2 , much larger than the largest
solid state and liquid transitions, which are about 10^{-15} cm^2 .[33] For
practical devices the latter figure seems a good upper bound. If we
then take A = 1μm x 10μm as an optimistically small laser cross
section (perhaps achievable by having the beam from one thin laser
intercept a second thin laser at a small angle), we calculate, for λ =
1μm, $h\nu = 2 \times 10^{-12}$ ergs

$$A/2\sigma = 10^{-7}/2 \times 10^{-15} = 5 \times 10^7$$
$$\tag{4-26}$$
$$P\tau = 10^{-4} \text{ ergs} = 10 \text{ picojoules}$$

This figure is a factor of 10 *smaller* than the lowest thresholds achieved
for GaAs injection lasers but still a factor of 30 *larger* than the $P\tau$
product quoted for field effect transistors in Chapter 2. Hence serial
optical logic can not be expected to become competitive with conventional semiconductor logic unless it demonstrates other advantages
not currently foreseen, or unless more promising logic embodiments
appear in the future. (Other embodiments have been proposed but
they do not seem to offer improvements.)

More promising than serial optical logic is serial optical data transmission, perhaps over optical fiber links. Already, experimental room
temperature injection lasers have threshold powers below 100 milliwatts.[34] Related devices, back biased p-n junctions,[35] also can be
used as polarization switches for the laser radiation, leading toward

the feasibility of miniaturized switches between optical fibers. The $P\tau$ product of such switches is expected to reach values still smaller than their present value of 100 picojoules. In nonminiaturized optical technology, a 10,000 megabits per second single channel optical pulse rate has already been achieved by time multiplexing techniques, using resonant polarization switches, applied to the nanosecond spaced 30 pico-second pulses of mode locked Nd YAG lasers.[36] It may be worth repeating that the attractiveness of lasers for commercial communications lies in the miniaturization possibility, and hence, the potential low cost and high spatial parallelism of the transmission, so that one can afford some tradeoff in the still unfavorable $P\tau$ product. For communications in outer space, it is the laser directionality that counts, and the miniaturization in question (with large high brightness lasers) can be visualized by comparing lenses and optical telescopes with microwave antennas and radio telescopes.

4.9 INPUT — OUTPUT; DISPLAY

The technological and systems aspects of the end points of an information processing system are quite different from those in the middle, and indeed are really not the theme of this book. However, optical technology obviously has strong branches dealing with interactions with man through his visual sense. These include scanning pictures or written or printed documents to convert the data contained therein to electronic form, and, at the other end of the data processing line, redisplaying the information in printed form or as a real time display with which the human being can interact. Familiar examples of such devices are typewriters, cathode ray displays as used in television, and means for multiplexing outputs such as printing presses or photocopiers.

Recent trends in the display area are summarized in reference 37. It is perhaps significant that lasers are given relatively little prominence in the survey, and only a limited role is seen for arrays of nonlasing electroluminescent diodes. However, as already noted, the time constant of various electro-optic materials such as liquid crystals and ferroelectric ceramics are compatible with their use in displays. The enduring cathode ray tube does seem to face increasing competition in the future. Some of the competition also comes from an equally enduring competitor, the localized gas discharge, which is graduating from simple nixie tubes to multi-electrode gas plasma displays.

Input-output applications of scanned laser beams other than display have also been slow to materialize, but are beginning to appear as commercial products. Here a wedding of mechanical and optical technology appears adequate. I.e., in a scanning mode, it is hard to beat the data throughput of a rotating mirror or prism for a one dimensional optical scan. Two dimensions may involve an independent mechanical motion such as paper displacement.

While mechanical technology seems adequate to many input-output applications, the fact that alternative electro-optic techniques have not long ago displaced mechanical ones in these fields is a discouraging measure of the weakness of electro-optic interactions.

4.10 SUMMARY

In summary, we have shown that there are two distinct trends influencing the evolution of optical technology. One is the same trend towards miniaturization and integration evident in the evolution of semiconductor and magnetic technology. The other is the availability of coherent light sources, important both for unsophisticated applications of intense focused optical energy and for more sophisticated applications of coherent optics. In some areas these trends supplement each other, but not all aspects of coherent optical technology or electro-optic control are compatible with miniaturization. This is especially true for high power and high radiance applications. Consequently there are some separate applications trends of miniaturized integrated optics and laser coherent optics. In the latter category we have not treated the field of precision measurement of distance, frequency and time or other measurement techniques such as holographic vibration analysis that provide new monitoring tools for technology. Incremental improvements such as the extension of the frequency range and sensitivity of optical detectors are also neglected.

REFERENCES

1. Kendall Preston, "Coherent Optical Computers," McGraw-Hill, N.Y. (1972).

2. A.R. Shulman, "Optical Data Processing," John Wiley & Sons, N.Y. (1970).

3. G.W. Stroke, "Optical Computing," IEEE Spectrum, 9, 12 (1972), 24–41.

4. William V. Smith, "Laser Applications," Artech House, Inc., Dedham, Mass. (1970), Chapters I–III.

5. Ibid, Chapter V.

6. "The Physics of Opto-Electronic Materials," ed. W.A. Albers, Jr., General Motors Symposia Series, Plenum Press, N.Y. (1971).

7. F-S Chen, "Modulators for Optical Communications," Proc. IEEE 58, 1440-1457 (1970).

8. C.E. Land and P.D. Thacher, "Modified Lead Zirconate Titanate Ceramics," Ref. 6, pp. 169–196. See also several articles in the 1972 Special Issues on

Applications of Ferroelectrics (papers from June 1971 Symposium on Applications held at the IBM T.J. Watson Research Center) published jointly by Ferroelectrics *3* and IEEE Transaction on Sonics and Ultrasonics, *SU-19*, (February and April issues respectively).

9.   J. Kobayashi, H. Schmid, and E. Ascher, "Optical Study on the Ferroelectric-Orthorhombic Phase of Fe-I-Boracite," Phys. Stat. Sol. *26*, 277–283 (1968).

10.   J. Kobayashi, I. Mitzutani, H. Schmid and H. Schachner, "X-ray Study on the Lattice Strains of Ferro-Electric Iron Iodine Boracite $Fe_3B_7O_{13}I$," Phys. Rev. *B1*, 3801-3808 (1970).

11.   H.N. Roberts, "Strain-Biased PLZT Input Devices (Page Composers) for Holographic Memories and Optical Data Processing," Applied Optics *11*, 397–404 (1972).

12.   J.R. Maldonado and L.K. Anderson, "Strain-Biased Ferroelectric-Photo-Conductor Image Storage and Display Devices Operated in a Reflection Mode," IEEE Trans. Electron. Devices *ED-18*, 774-777 (1971).

13.   R.W. Dixon, "The Acousto-Optic Interaction," Ref. 6, pp. 131–149.

14.   D.A. Pinnow, "Acousto-Optic Light Deflection: Design Considerations for First Order Beam Steering Transducers," IEEE Trans. on Sonics and Ultrasonics, *SU-18*, (1971) 209-214. See also D.A. Pinnow, L.G. Van Uitert, A. W. Warner, and W.A. Bonner, "Lead Molybdate: A Melt-grown Crystal with a High Figure of Merit for Acousto-optic Device Applications," App. Phys. Lett. *15*, 83–86 (1969).

15.   R.A. Soref, "Liquid-Crystal Light-Control Experiments," Ref. 6 pp. 207–231.

16.   D. Adler and J. Feinleib, "Optics of Solid State Phase Transformations," Ref. 6, pp. 233–253.

17.   I.P. Kaminow, J.R. Carruthers, E.H. Turner, and L.W. Stutz. "Thin-film $LiNbO_3$ electro-optic light modulator," Appl. Phys. Lett. *22*, 540–542 (1973).

18.   T. Uchida, M. Furukawa, I. Kitano, K. Koizumi, and H. Matsumura, "Optical Characteristics of a Light-Focusing Fiber Guide and Its Applications," IEEE J. Quant. Electron. *QE-6*, 606–612 (1970).

19.   D. Gloge, "Optical Waveguide Transmission," Proc. IEEE *58*, 1513–22 (1970).

20.   T.W. Hänsch, F. Varsanyi, and A.L. Schawlow, "Image Amplification by Dye Lasers," Appl. Phys. Lett. *18*, 108–110 (1971).

21.   F.P. Kapron, D.B. Keck, and R.D. Maurer, "Radiation Losses in Glass Optical Waveguides," Appl. Phys. Lett. *17*, 423–425 (1970).

22.   O.E. deLange, "Wide-Band Optical Communications Systems: Part II-Frequency Division Multiplexing," Proc. IEEE *58*, 1683–1690 (1970).

23.   W.V. Smith, ref. 4, Chapter 4. See also the references contained therein

and E.S. Barrekette et.al., eds. "Applications of Holography, Plenum, N.Y., 1971.

24. O.N. Tufte and D. Chen, "Optical Techniques for Data Storage," IEEE Spectrum *10*, Feb. 1973, pp. 26–32.

25. T.C. Lee, "MnBi Film as Potential Storage Media in Holographic Optical Memories," Applied Optics *11*, 384–389 (1972).

26. J.A. Rajchman, "Promise of Optical Memories," J. Appl. Phys. *41*, 1376–1383 (1970).

27. J.J. Amodei, W. Phillips, and D.L. Staebler, "Improved Electro-Optic Materials and Fixing Techniques for Holographic Recording," Applied Optics *11*, 390–396 (1972).

28. H.J. Caufield, D.J. McMahon and R.A. Soref, "Stacked Hologram Apparatus," United States Patent 3,635,538, Jan. 18, 1972.

29. J.C. Marinace, "Experimental Fabrication of One-dimensional GaAs Laser Arrays," IBM J. Res. Develop. *15*, 258–264 (1971); G.J. Sprokel, "Fabrication and Properties of Monolithic Laser Diode Arrays," Ibid, 265–271 (1971).

30. G.J. Lasher and A.B. Fowler, "Mutually Quenched Injection Lasers as Bistable Devices," IBM J. Res. Develop. *8*, 471–475 (1964)

31. W.V. Smith, ref. 4, Chapter 6.

32. R.W. Keyes, "Nonlinear Absorbers of Light," IBM J. Res. Develop. 7, 334–336 (1963).

33. An example is $o = 0.4 \times 10^{-15} \, cm^2$ for Rhodamine B or 6G [O.G. Peterson, J.P. Webb, and W.C. McColgin, J. Appl. Phys. *42*, 1917-28 (1971)].

34. T.Tsukada, H. Nadashima, J. Umeda, S. Nakamuro, N. Chinone, R. Ito, and O. Nadada, "Very-Low-Current Operation of Mesa-Stripe-Geometry Double-Heterostructure Injection Lasers," Appl. Phys. Lett. *20*, 344-345 (1972).

35. K. F. Reinhart and B.I. Miller, "Efficient GaAs-Al$_x$ Ga$_{1-x}$ As Double Hetero-structure Light Modulators," Appl. Phys. Lett. *20*, 36–38 (1972).

36. T.S. Kinsel, "Wide-Band Optical Communications Systems: Part I — Time Division Multiplexing," Proc. IEEE *58*, 1666-1683 (1970).

37. See, for instance, the Special Issue on Information Display Devices, IEEE Trans. On Electron Devices, *ED–18*, September 1971.

PROBLEMS

4.1 Using Eq. (4-1) as a guide.

a. Comment on how faithfully a 1 mm wide grating consisting of sharp 1 μm wide grooves cut in a thin film can be imaged at unity magnification by an f8 lens, 1 cm in diameter, under illumination by a collimated laser beam, $\lambda = 0.5\ \mu$m. (f8 refers to the ratio of focal length to lens diameter.)

b.   What would be the result for an f0.8 lens, all other parameters remaining the same?

4.2 Contrast the deflection capabilities of the acousto-optic deflector discussed following Eq. (4-18) with an electrostatic cathode ray deflector of the same dimensions.

a.   What is the transit time of a 1 kilovolt electron beam through the long dimension?

b.   What transverse velocity is transmitted to the beam at the end of its transit through the deflector by 30 volts applied across the plates?

c.   How far is the beam deflected at the end of the plates? After a further 20 cm path length?

d.   Compare c. with the maximum deflection of the optical deflector.

4.3 Optical fibers are miniaturized low loss optical transmission lines. The simplest type consist of a core material perhaps 10 μm in diameter, clad by a 100 μm diameter sheath with an index of refraction perhaps 0.75% less than that of the core. Since the core is several wavelengths in diameter it can support many modes of propagation subject only to the restriction that the light remain totally internally reflected. This determines an acceptance core angle for the rays $\Phi^2 \cong 2\Delta\ n/n$

a.   What f-number lens can focus the entire output of a perfectly collimated laser within the acceptance angle of the above described optical fiber. (Assume $n \cong 1.5$)

b.   In a 1 kilometer length of the fiber, what is the relative time delay between that part of an optical signal propagating directly along the core axis and that suffering the maximum number of internal reflections?

4.4 The constant of proportionality in Eq. (4-10) can be put in a form proportional to wd/ℓ, where w and d are the transverse dimensions of the crystal modulator. However these dimensions are independent variables *only* if diffraction spread of the light can be neglected. For bulk modulators this spread cannot be neglected, resulting in a limitation $d^2/\ell = S^2\ (4\lambda/n\Pi)$ with a safety factor $S \geqslant 3$, for the case w = d. For planar integrated optics, spreading transverse to the d dimension is avoided by the trapped light. For an optical fiber light is trapped in two dimensions.

a.   For example of Eq. (4-11) w = d = 0.25mm and ℓ = 10mm. What value of $P\tau$ could be anticipated for a planar structure leaving W/L unchanged, but reducing d to 1μm?

b.   Why is $P\tau$ for ref. 17 so much larger than this value?

c.   Why is $P\tau$ for a back biased p-n junction modulator in a GaA_1As also larger than anticipated from the above argument (ref..35).

d.   What would $P\tau$ be idealy for an optical fiber scaled from Eq. (4-11) with w = d = 1μm and ℓ = 100μm.

4.5   We may visualize a three dimensional hologram as a superposition of three dimensional gratings. We may estimate the intensity of laser light scattered from one of these gratings by adding up all the reflected rays from the N multilayer structure: $I = I_0 \left(\dfrac{\sin N z}{\sin z} \right)^2$, where z is the phase difference between successive rays.

Consider, for example the case for back reflection, $\theta = \Pi$, Eq. (4-20), and $z = \Pi$. The intensity drops to half its maximum for a shift Δz in the phase given by

$$N^2 I_0 = I_0 \left(\frac{\sin N (\Delta z/2)}{\sin (\Delta z/2)} \right)^2 \text{ or, approximately}$$

$$\Delta z = \sqrt{2/N}$$

This phase difference can be related to the angular shift $\Delta\theta$ at the half intensity point since

$$\Delta z = \Pi - \frac{\Pi}{2} (1 + \cos \Delta\theta) = \frac{\pi\Delta\theta^2}{4}$$

Similarly, for $\Delta\theta = 0$, a wavelength resolution $\Delta\lambda \approx \dfrac{\lambda}{N}$ can be derived.

Use the above relations to make plausible the statement that a volume hologram can store an amount of information approaching V/λ^3. (Assume these relations hold for any value of θ in Eq. (4-20).)

4.6   A laser is an amplifier of light with feedback for oscillation provided by mirrors at the ends of the laser of length ℓ. When oscillating the product of the exponential gain, $e^{g\ell}$ and the reflectivity loss R equals unity: $Re^{g\ell} = 1$, where $g = n\sigma$, n being the "population inversion" of the medium. For example, in a semiconductor laser, n is the number of electron-hole pairs per unit volume which can recombine with the emission of near band gap radiation.

The gain equation above neglects spontaneous emission. However, the *threshold* for stimulated laser emission can be estimated by recognizing that an external power source must provide *at least* the power for spontaneous emission this criterion is

$P = nVh\nu/\tau,$

where τ is the radiative recombination time.

For a GaAs laser, $\lambda = 0.9\mu m$, σ is approximately 3×10^{-15} cm^2 and R, provided by Fresnel reflection of the GaAs=air boundary, 0.3. What are the

a.   Theoretical population inversion?

b. $P\tau$ product for a laser of dimensions $1 \times 10 \times 100 \mu m$, lasing in the long dimension?

c.   For an injection laser, the population inversion is achieved by passing current through the p-n junction:

$j/ed = n/\tau$

Where d is the small dimension of the laser, j the current density, and we have assumed 100% quantum efficiency. For GaAs, $\tau = 10^{-9}$ seconds. What current density is required at the laser threshold?

Superconductivity

In contrast to the situation for the technologies discussed in Chapters 2 through 5, no commercial products in the information processing field exist today that make use of superconducting technology. However there are other commercial uses of superconducting technology including the emerging field of very sensitive and precise laboratory instrumentation. Moreover, theoretical and experimental investigations have established the fact that Josephson junction superconducting switching phenomena are among the fastest electronic phenomena observed, and certainly have the lowest power dissipation. This chapter explores the possibility of making use of these phenomena for information processing.

The 1972 and 1973 Nobel Prize awards, to J. Bardeen, L.N. Cooper, and J.R. Schrieffer, and to L. Esaki, I. Giaver, and B.D. Josephson, respectively, are measures of the progress, excitement and promise of the fields of superconductivity and electron tunneling through thin junctions, fields which merge in the explorations of this chapter.

Superconductivity has made an entrance into industrial applications only in the last decade. The entrance is along a broad front, however. Superconducting magnets are well established commercially.[1, 2] Research is well advanced in motors and generators employing superconductive windings, in superconducting power transmission,[3] and in superconducting resonant cavities used in high energy particle accelerators for nuclear physics.[4] These applications all employ physically large superconducting circuits in which they make maximum use of the lossless current flow that is the most dramatic, and first observed, property of superconductivity. Within this same decade, however, two new but related phenomena, quantized flux storage and Josephson tunneling, have been observed in relatively small superconducting circuits and have led to a wide variety of sensitive measuring instruments: magnetometers, voltmeters, ammeters, and high-frequency detectors.[5-7] These effects have also provided

101

new and improved ways of measuring a particular combination of
atomic constants, e/h.[8, 9] In this section we shall be concerned with
a few examples of devices based on these phenomena which have
been proposed and are being investigated for their data-processing
capabilities. We shall see that our requirements of circuit miniaturization and speed maximization pose rather different constraints on
the parameters of interest than those posed by maximizing measuring sensitivity.

5.1   CRYOTRON MEMORY AND LOGIC CONCEPTS

The concept of storing information in the persistent circulating currents of superconducting circuits was introduced by D.A. Buck in
1956,[10] before the discoveries of the flux quantization and Josephson
tunneling phenomena on which the present concepts of these devices
are based. An elementary cryotron flip-flop circuit demonstrating
the principle involved is shown in Fig. 5-1.

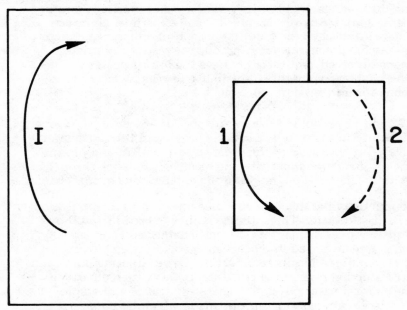

Figure 5-1.   Cryotron Circuit
Circuit supercurrent I can be switched from branch 1
to branch 2 by temporarily destroying the superconductivity in branch 1.

A circulating current stored in the major loop of Fig. 5-1 can be
shuttled from branch 1 to branch 2 by control circuits (not shown)

that temporarily destroy the superconductivity in branch 1. (This is
done by generating a pulsed magnetic field to drive a portion of the
superconductor into its normal resistance state.) Attractive features
of this technology included the facts that it could be integrated on
surfaces, that both logic and memory functions could be accomplished
with the same technology,[10, 11] and that the memory function did not
dissipate power. A disadvantage, of course, was and is the requirement of low temperature operation; however this was not the obstacle
that killed this first family of superconducting computer devices. The
practical limitations of these devices were set by the fact that the
superconducting — normal conductivity transition proved to be a
relatively slow phase change, with time constant typically 40-50 nanoseconds.[12]

The present, second, round of interest in superconducting computer
elements was sparked by Juri Matisoo's observation[13] that if a Josephson junction, i.e., an insulating layer of a few tens of angstroms thickness sandwiched between two superconducting surfaces, was incorporated in each arm of the circuit, it was sufficient to switch *the junction*
between its superconducting and nonsuperconducting states (see Section
5-4) rather than to switch a portion of the bulk superconductor.
Matisoo's first experiments demonstrated an upper bound of 800
picoseconds for the switching speed of the junction, and this bound
has subsequently been reduced to 85ps,[14] with the expectation of
substantial further reductions. Hence, speed is no longer a limitation,
but rather a potential advantage of superconducting technology.
Meanwhile, the advances in other cryogenic applications have made the
requirement of low temperature operation a less formidable obstacle
than it once seemed. On the other hand, however, competing technologies have also advanced, and the integration of logic and memory
in one technology has also been achieved in other technologies — semiconductors, for instance (Chapter 2). We shall not seek to predict the
ultimate outcome of the competition, but will try to describe the
superconducting approach sufficiently that the reader can make his
own comparisons.

5.2 PHYSICAL BASIS OF SUPERCONDUCTIVITY

Electrical conduction in metals al all but the lowest temperatures can
be understood on the basis of the uncorrelated motion of individual
electrons. However, there are attractive and repulsive forces between
electrons that tend to correlate their motion and in many metals at
very low temperatures these overcome the randomizing effects of
thermal motion. The overall charge neutrality of a metal is highly
asymmetric and time dependent on a local scale: a negative electron
moving at or near the Fermi velocity of about 10^8 cm/sec drags a
positive space charge lattice distortion in its wake. This positive space

charge, in turn, attracts other electrons and, in particular, attract most strongly electrons moving in the same line. Since the Pauli principle excludes pairing electrons with identical positions and vector velocities, it is electrons with opposing vector velocities that are most strongly attracted to each other. As a consequence, an energy gap 2Δ opens up in the electron density of states between the uncorrelated single electrons and the paired electrons.[15, 16] Moreover, it turns out that the spatial extent of these electron pairs is so large that many of these pairs overlap in the same space, and a microscopic correlation of electron momenta takes place. The resulting condensed phase is superconducting below a critical temperature T_c, where the simplest theoretical approximation gives [16]

$$2\Delta_0 \cong 3.5kT_c \tag{5-1}$$

as the value of the energy gap at $0°K$. Table 5-1 shows a few measured values of 2Δ and T_c. They lie in the ranges of a few millivolts and a few degrees Kelvin, respectively, with the highest reported value of T_c only slightly above $20°K$.

Table 5-1
Superconducting Energy Gaps,
Transition Temperatures, and Critical Fields[17]

Material	$T_c °K$	$\dfrac{2\Delta_0}{e}$ (millivolts)	H_0 (gauss)
Sn	3.722	1.1	304
Pb	7.21	2.7	803
Nb	9.2	2.9	1960

The energy gap may also be related to a limiting frequency, f, max, above which absorption of a photon converts an electron pair into two uncorrelated electrons, or "quasi-particles." The relation is

$$f\max = 2\Delta/h = 2.42 \times 10^{11} \text{ Hz/millivolt} \tag{5-2}$$

A typical superconducting density of states is shown in Fig. 5-2A. It is clear that if the upper frequency limit of superconducting circuits is determined by Eq. (5-2), energy gaps of a few millivolts are sufficient to achieve time constants of the order of picoseconds.

Electronic motion is affected by magnetic fields and, indeed, magnetic fields above a critical value H_c destroy superconductivity. In some materials superconductivity is gradually destroyed over a range of critical fields H_{c1}, H_{c2}, and H_{c3}, with various hysteresis properties associated with the subscripts. These hysteresis effects are very important for high field superconducting magnets, but not for the relatively low critical field materials with which we are concerned; see Table (5-1).

Figure 5-2A. Electron Density of States in a Superconductor
The Fermi level is shown in the middle of the gap 2Δ opened up by the pairing mechanism. At $0°$ K, states below E_f are full and paired, states above E_f are empty.

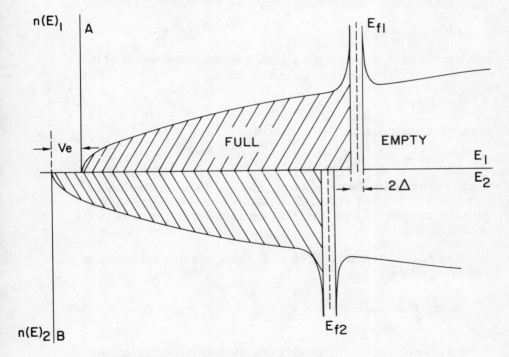

Figure 5-2B. Superconductive Tunneling Possibilities Across a Junction
Density of states $n(E_2)$ is displaced by Ve from $n(E_1)$ by application of a voltage V across a junction between two identical superconductors. If V = 0 the gaps are aligned and dc pair tunneling is possible. If $Ve > 2\Delta$, single quasi-particles can tunnel from full band in 1 to empty band in 2. For $0 < Ve < 2\Delta$, ac pair tunneling takes place.

Finally, the parameters Δ and H_c are both monotonic functions of temperature, with their maximum values at $T = 0$, and vanishing at $T = T_c$. Their initial temperature dependencies are not marked, however, and only close to T_c do they drop off sharply.

5.3 FLUX QUANTIZATION AND ENERGY STORAGE

One of the exciting scientific events of 1961 was Deaver and Fairbank's and Doll and Näbauer's discovery of the quantization of magnetic flux in superconductors,[18] originally predicted by London.[19] In essence, the angular momentum $\vec{P}$ associated with a constant circulating current and flux in a closed superconducting ring is quantized:

$$\oint \vec{P} \cdot \vec{d\ell} = N h \qquad (5\text{-}3)$$

where $N = 0$ or an integer. But the momentum is the center of mass momentum of the circulating paired electrons:

$$\vec{P} = h\nabla\gamma = 2(mv_{cm} + e\vec{A}) \qquad (5\text{-}4)$$

where $\vec{A}$ is the magnetic vector potential,

$$\nabla \times \vec{A} = \vec{B} = \mu_o \vec{H}, \qquad (5\text{-}5)$$

m and e the charge of each electron, and v_{cm} their center of mass velocity. The left half of Eq. (5-4) relates $\vec{P}$ to the phase γ of the quantum mechanical wave function associated with the paired electrons.

Inserting Eqs. (5-4) and (5-5) in (5-3), then, the flux contained in the circulating ring is

$$\Phi = \iint_S \vec{B} \cdot \vec{ds} = \oint \vec{A} \cdot \vec{d\ell} = \frac{h}{2e} N - \frac{m}{e} \oint \vec{v}_{cm} \cdot \vec{d\ell} \qquad (5\text{-}6)$$

where $\oint$ indicates a line integral around the superconducting loop. The integral may be carried out over a path within the superconductor where $\vec{v}_{cm} = 0$ (no current penetration), hence the flux is quantized:

$$\Phi = N \Phi_0; \Phi_0 = \frac{h}{2e} = 2.07 \times 10^{-7} \text{ Gaus cm}^2 = 20.7 G \,\mu m^2 \qquad (5\text{-}7)$$

Let us now examine the magnetic field H and stored energy E in the superconducting loop of Fig. 5-3, a short stripline of length ℓ, width

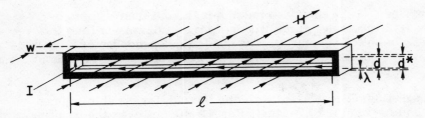

Figure 5-3. Quantized Flux Storage
The magnetic flux threading a superconducting circuit is
quantized in units of $\Phi = 20.7\ G\mu m^2$. In the parallel
plate transmission line shown $\Phi \approx \ell d^* \times H$, with $d^* = d$
$d + 2\lambda$, where λ is the penetration depth. The current
flow I is restricted to a depth approximately equal to λ.

w, and "effective" separation d* (a term that includes an allowance
for the penetration of the flux a distance λ into each superconductor).
London's theoretical approximation, λ_L, of the distance, several times
smaller than experimental valves, is [19]

$$\lambda_L = (m/\mu\rho e^2)^{-1/2} \tag{5-8}$$

with ρ the density of electron pairs. The spatial variation of the magnetic field follows the relation

$$\nabla^2 \vec{H} = \lambda^{-2}\vec{H}. \tag{5-9}$$

and is of the order of 10^{-5} cm for most materials. It has been
measured to be about 450 A for lead film.[20]

If the stripline spacing is thin enough so that H is effectively uniform
over the cross section,

$$B = \Phi/\ell d^* = 20.7N/\ell d^*\ \text{Gauss} \tag{5-10}$$

$$E = \frac{10^{-7}\ \ell wd^*}{8\pi}\ H^2 = 1.7 \times 10^{-6} N^2 w/\ell d^*\ \text{picojoules} \tag{5-11}$$

where we have chosen to use the mixed units of gauss, micrometers,
and picojoules.

In Eqs. (5-10) and the right hand form of (5-11), ℓ and d* occur in
the denominator, thus pursuing miniaturization to extremes may
make E and B undesirably large. However micrometer dimensions
pose no serious problems. For instance, we may take d* = 0.5μm
(well above the penetration depth limit of 0.1μm). For an aspect

ratio w/ℓ of 1/3, the energy stored in one fluxoid then is approximately 10^{-6} picojoules, three orders of magnitude smaller than for magnetic bubbles (Chapter 3). The quadratic dependence of E on N shows that devices requiring a large number of fluxoids show a rapid increase in energy storage.

The magnetic field associated with one fluxoid, for the above dimensions, and $\ell = 2\mu m$ is 20.7 Gauss. For N = 40, however, the resulting 828 Gauss would be enough to destroy superconductivity in lead! Fortunately a smaller number of flux quanta should be adequate.

5.4 THE dc JOSEPHSON EFFECT

If two superconductors are separated by a thin insulating layer — generally a grown oxide — with thickness t of only a few tens of angstroms, the paired superconducting electrons can tunnel through the junction at zero voltage. This behaviour was predicted by Josephson,[21] for whom the device is named, and experimentally confirmed by Anderson and Rowell.[22] Above a maximum current, I_{max}, the superconductivity of the junction (not the electrodes) is destroyed, but single particle normal tunneling continues. More accurately for $I > I_{max}$, the supercurrent I_p and the normal "quasi-particle" current I_q flow in parallel with a nonlinear I-V characteristic given by Fig. 5-4. The junction superconductivity is destroyed at a current somewhat less that that where I_q becomes linear: i.e.,[23]

$$I_{max} \approx I_q \ (2\Delta) \text{ or more exactly}$$

$$I_{max} = [\pi\Delta(T)/2eR_{NT}] \ \tanh \ [\Delta(T)/2kT] \qquad (5\text{-}12)$$

where $2\Delta(T)$ is the temperature-dependent superconducting energy gap and R_{NT} is the temperature-independent normal tunneling resistance of the junction. Fig. 5-2 shows the density of states curves for two identical superconductors, one displaced relative to the other by the energy Ve corresponding to a voltage V applied across the junction. When the energy gaps coincide (V = 0) dc supercurrent tunneling occurs, and quasi-particle tunneling occurs when full states in 1 can tunnel to empty states in 2. The situation at T = 0 where there is no thermal tailing of the filling of the states is shown.

Eq. (5-12) and Fig. 5-4 shows that a prerequisite to estimating the maximum tunneling supercurrent, I_{max}, is a knowledge of the normal tunneling current I_q. To a good approximation, at low temperatures, this current is linear in the voltage (above 2Δ) and hence the junction indeed can be characterized by a normal tunneling resistivity R_{NT}. R_{NT} has an exponential dependence on insulator thickness and metal

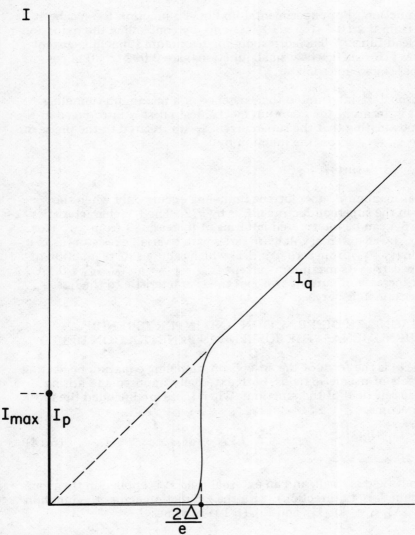

Figure 5-4. Josephson Tunneling

Supercurrent pair tunneling current I_p flows at zero voltage across a sufficiently thin junction up to a maximum value I_{max} given by Eq. (12). For $I > I_{max}$ the junction switches to the quasi-particle tunneling curve I_q which is linear in V for $V > 2\Delta/e$. When V is lowered, the current shows hysteresis, dropping to a low value for for $V < 2\Delta/e$. (This corresponds to an absence of empty states for tunneling from full band in Fig. 2.)

work function. For experimental Pb-PbO-Pb junction R_N has been varied from 2×10^{-7} to 5×10^{-3} Ω cm^2 by controlling the oxidation of the lead films.[20] The corresponding maximum tunneling current densities j (for sufficiently small junctions) are 0.002 to 50 mico-amps per square micrometer.

Josephson[21, 24] interpreted the existence of a maximum tunneling current in terms of the quantum mechanical phase γ introduced in Eq. (5-4), postulating that the supercurrent I_P was related to the phase difference $\gamma_1 - \gamma_2$ across the junction by

$$I_p = I_{max} \sin(\gamma_1 - \gamma_2) \tag{5-13}$$

i.e., that maximum supercurrent tunneling occurs only when the phases in the superconductors differ by $\pi/2$. The I-V characteristics of Fig. 5-4 can be interpreted in terms of increasing I from zero (for instance, by an external voltage in series with a variable resistor) as an increase in $(\gamma_1 - \gamma_2)$ from zero to $\pi/2$, at which value a square junction of width w carries its maximum current $I_{max} = j_0 w^2$ at $V_{junction} = 0$. A further increase of current switches the characteristic to the quasi-particle tunneling curve at $V_j \approx 2\Delta/e$.

5.5 MAGNETIC DIFFRACTION AND INTERFERENCE PHENOMENA; THE JOSEPHSON PENETRATION DEPTH

Eq. (5-13) is the form of the Josephson tunneling equation neglecting the effects of magnetic fields, both externally imposed and arising from the self field of the junction. When these are included the relation becomes

$$j_m = j_0 \sin\left\{\gamma_1 - \gamma_2 - \frac{2e}{h} \int_1^2 \vec{A} \cdot \vec{d\ell}\right\} \tag{5-14}$$

If the self field is small, and an external field H is applied in the plane of the junction, (x direction), with the z direction across the junction (Fig. 5-5A), $\vec{A} = \hat{k}\mu_0 Hx$ and Eq. (5-14) becomes

$$j_m = j_0 \sin\left\{(\gamma_1 - \gamma_2)_{x=0} - \frac{2ed^*\mu_0 x}{h}\right\} \tag{5-15}$$

setting $\gamma_1 - \gamma_2$ at its maximum value of $\pi/2$ and integrating across the junction to $x = \ell(\ell \gg w)$ results in the Fraunhofer diffraction relation

$$I_m = I_{max} (\sin \pi\Phi_J/\Phi_0 / \pi\Phi_J/\Phi_0) \tag{5-16}$$

shown in Fig. 5-5B. Here $\Phi_J = \ell d^*\mu_0 H$ is the magnetic flux thread-

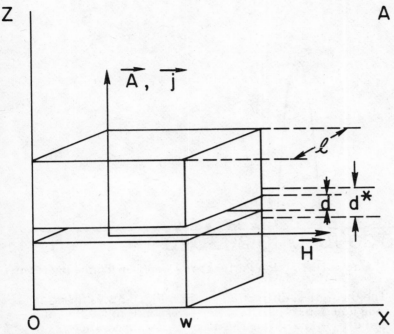

Figure 5-5. Magnetic Diffraction Pattern for Josephson Tunneling
In switching devices the geometry resembles Fig. 5-5A,
with the junction length $\ell \cong$ its width w, and a flux link-
age $H\ell d^*$ ($d^* = d + 2\lambda$). The magnetic vector potential $\vec{A}$
and current $\vec{j}$ are perpendicular to the junction plane
threaded by $\vec{H}$.

ing the junction and Φ_0 the flux quantum already introduced in our
discussion of flux quantization. A qualitatively similar expression
holds for the square junctions $\ell = w$ of practical interest.

Fig. 5-5 shows that one way to switch a Josephson junction from its
supercurrent to its normal tunneling current state is to apply an external field sufficient to reduce I_m below the current in the circuit
(assumed driven by a constant current source). Eq. (5-16) shows that
I_m is reduced to its first zero when the junction contains one flux
quantum. At this point the phase difference varies by a full period
across the junction plane, which, therefore, carries cancelling supercurrents, flowing in opposite directions, in its two halves. Substituting
in Eq. (5-10) a typical junction value

$$d^* \approx 2\lambda = 0.1\,\mu m \qquad\qquad (5\text{-}17)$$

with $\ell = 2\,\mu m$ yields a value of 100 gauss for this first zero.

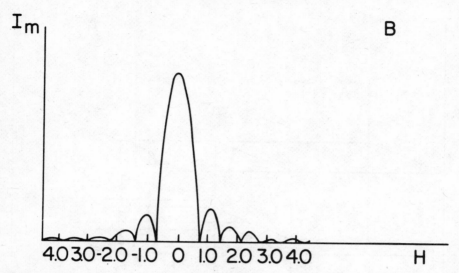

Figure 5-5.   Magnetic Diffraction Pattern for Josephson Tunneling (cont.)

> The theoretical diffraction pattern, Fig. 5-5B, is for a
> long junction, $\ell \gg w$. Its scale corresponds to $\ell = 250\mu$m
> and $d^* = 0.12\mu$, giving the magnetic field periodicity
> shown, in agreement with experiment[29].

If two junctions are incorporated in a superconducting loop, one in
each arm of the minor loop of Fig. 5-1 for instance, the maximum
current through both junctions yields an interference pattern whose
maxima are given by the flux quantization condition of Eq. (5-7).
More generally, using Eqs. (5-3) and (5-4) to determine $\gamma_1 - \gamma_2$ across
the junction for a given current density

$$j = 2\rho\, ev_{cm} \tag{5-18}$$

Eq. (5-14) then yields the interference relations

$$I'_m = 2I_m\, \cos\pi\Phi_L/\Phi_0 \tag{5-19}$$

where Φ_L is the flux threading the loop, and I_p is the maximum supercurrent through each junction, assumed identical, given by Eq. (5-16).
Similar relations hold for a single junction in the loop.

Eq. (5-19) is the basis for a broad class of sensitive measuring instruments since, for a large loop, the periodic zeros of integral flux quanta
correspond to very small magnetic field increments — 0.2 microgauss
for one cm² area. However, in miniaturized switching circuits, these

interference phenomena may represent an undesirable complication in achieving uniform magnetic field control characteristics of the junctions. If the number of flux quanta in the loop is relatively large, the depth of modulation of the interference is small enough not to present a problem. Presumably the interference can also be controlled in the other extreme when N is very small.

Finally, the magnetic field of the tunneling circuit can also be important. In this case the phase across the junction follows the relation[24]

$$\frac{\partial^2 \gamma}{\partial x^2} + \frac{\partial^2 \gamma}{\partial y^2} = \lambda_J^{-2} \sin \gamma \tag{5-20}$$

where

$$\lambda_J = \left(\frac{h}{2e\mu \, d^* j} \right)^{1/2} \tag{5-21}$$

is the Josephson penetration depth, i.e., the distance in from the junction edge to which most of the current flow is restricted. This effect can be neglected for small junctions,[20]

$$w < 2 \lambda_J \tag{5-22}$$

In Eq. (5-21), using $d^* = 0.1 \mu m$ Eq. (5-17) and $j_0 = 10 \mu A/\mu m^2$ predicts a value of λ_J of $5 \mu m$, compared to an observed range of 10 to 20 μm in one group of experiments[25]. Thus we see that pursuing miniaturization to its logical conclusion will result in automatically satisfying the current uniformity criterion of Eq. (5-22).

5.6 THE ac JOSEPHSON EFFECT

So far we have only discussed supercurrent tunneling at zero voltage drop across the junction. Can the junction support a voltage drop and, if so, what happens to the supercurrent? Josephson also answered this question with the prediction of the ac Josephson effect, adding to Eq. (5-14) or (5-15) the relation

$$\frac{\partial}{\partial t} (\gamma_1 - \gamma_2) = \frac{2e}{h} V \tag{5-23}$$

where V is the voltage drop across the junction. For a fixed voltage and uniform phase along the junction, then,

$$\gamma_1 - \gamma_2 = \frac{2e}{\hbar} Vt = \omega t$$

where　　　　　　　　　　　　　　　　　　　　　　　　　(5-24)

$$\omega = \left(\frac{2e}{\hbar} \right) V$$

This is in fact the same quantum relation as Eq. (5-2), replacing the half energy gap Δ by V, but the interpretation is different. For V less than 2Δ, application of a constant voltage generates an alternating supercurrent of frequency $\omega/2\pi$, whereas applying a frequency above $\frac{2e}{\hbar}$ breaks up the superconducting electron pairs.

Eq. (5-24) and analogous relations combining the effects of superimposed dc and ac voltages are the basis of a second class of electronic instruments for generating, detecting, and mixing very high frequency currents. It is also the basis of a voltage standard based on accurate frequency standards, and of a precise measurement of e/h. For our purpose, it also modifies the transient behavior of supercurrent switching devices and raises the possibility that the high frequency limit after all may not be set by Eq. (5-2) since ac Josephson effect ringing phenomena must also be taken into account. Such an analysis is beyond the scope of this chapter.

5.7 DEVICES

The previous sections have described a rich set of phenomena of superconductivity. Most of these have already been exploited in a variety of sensitive measuring techniques. To date only two of these phenomena, flux quantization and the dc Josephson effect — considered together — have been proposed for data processing applications. Since these proposals are in an exploratory research stage as contrasted with the advanced development and actual systems use stages of at least some realizations of more traditional technologies, our discussion is necessarily sketchy and incomplete.

Two somewhat related types of devices have been proposed. In both cases the controlling element of the device is a Josephson junction which is switched from its quasi-particle tunneling state. Consider, for example, the circuit of Fig. 5-1, with Josephson junctions J_1 and J_2 in branches 1 and 2 respectively. Let J_2 be biased by a control magnetic field to reduce I_m to zero, thus establishing the supercurrent flow in branch 1. Switching the control field from branch 2 to 1 will switch the supercurrent from branch 1 to 2. The operation is essentially the same as that of earlier cryotron flip-flop circuits, and similar circuit layouts using superconducting strip lines over superconducting ground planes can be used. Fig. 5-6 shows part of a min-

Figure 5-6. Scanning electron micrograph of an array of Josephson junctions, the smallest with dimensions of about 1.3×7 micron square. Figure courtesy of IBM.

iaturized array of such circuits. New circuits are also possible. The control magnetic fields are also generated by strip lines, and have gain so that they can perform logic operations. This is the generic circuit and method of operation proposed by Matisoo[13]. In one experiment using rather large junctions[28] (10 mil diameter) and a long 1.16 inch loop, he transferred a 20mA current from one branch to the other in less than 2 nanoseconds, a time determined by the loop inductance ($L = 1.08 \times 10^{-10}$H). The control pulse was 2mA, i.e., a current gain of ten. Subsequent experiments[14] using somewhat smaller junctions ($100 \mu m \times 125 \mu m$) and a somewhat shorter transmission line (1cm) achieved a 550ps cycle time, and one would anticipate further improvement with further miniaturization. Note that the time limitations here are imposed by the circuit and have not yet reached the limit imposed by the junction switching time, less than 85ps[14] experimentally. The theoretical limits imposed by the frequency of absorption across the gap (Eq. (5-21)) or the ac Josephson effect (Eq. (5-24)) have yet to be reached.

A second type of superconducting circuit, more akin to magnetic bubble memory than to logic devices, has been proposed by Anderson[7, 26]. He suggests shunting a superconducting transmission line by an equally spaced series of identical Josephson junctions, thereby providing a ladder of storage loops for individual flux quanta. No detailed description of the switching circuits is given, but the general idea is to pulse the current through one junction above I_{max}, thereby destroying its superconductivity, and therefore necessarily transferring any flux stored in a loop embracing the junction to a different loop. Continuing work in the field will presumably lead to still other basic circuits, perhaps capitalizing on other superconducting phenomena.

Whether or not this exploratory research will lead to an actual technology of integrated superconducting data processing circuits depends on many factors, analysis of which is beyond the scope of this book. Certainly the speed and low power dissipation potentials exist, but the technology must also be cheap and reliable to compete with present technology.

REFERENCES

1. J.K. Hulm, D.J. Kasun and E. Mullan, "Superconducting Magnets," Phys. Today 24, No. 8, 48–57 (August, 1971).

2. See, for example, the sections on Magnets, special section on Applied Superconductivity, J. Appl. Phys. 39, 2622–2652 (1968); ibid 40 2101–2110 (1969), and ibid 42, 59–81 (1971).

3. See section on Power, ibid 42, 10–26 (1971).

4. See section on High-Frequency Resonators and Lines, ibid 42, 82–106 (1971).

5. B.N. Taylor, "Device Applications of Superconductive Tunneling," ibid 39, 2490–2502, (1968).

6. Section on Quantum Interference Devices, ibid 42, 27–45 (1971).

7. J. Clarke, "Electronics with Superconducting Junctions," Phys. Today 24, No. 48, 30-37 (August 1971).

8. D.N. Langenberg, W.H. Parker and B.N. Taylor, "Experimental Test of the Josephson Frequency-Voltage Relation," Phys. Rev. 150, 186–188 (1966).

9. J. Clarke, "The Josephson Effect and e/h," Am. J. Phys. 38, 1071–1095 (1970).

10. D.A. Buck, "The Cryotron — A Superconductive Computer Component," Proc. IRE, *44*, 482–493 (1956).

11. See section on Computer Devices, special section on Applied Superconductivity, J. Appl. Phys. *39*, 2579–2591 (1968).

12. A.E. Brenneman, H. Saki and D.P. Seraphim, "Dynamic Operation of the In-Line Cryotron in Bistable Circuits," Proc. IEEE *52*, 228–238 (1964).

13. J. Matisoo, "Subnanosecond Pair Tunneling Single Particle Tunneling Transitions in Josephson Junctions," Appl. Phys. Lett. *9*, 167–168 (1966); "The Tunneling Cryotron — A Superconductive Logic Element Based on Electron Tunneling," Proc. IEEE *55*, 172–180 (1967).

14. H.H. Zappe and K.R. Grebe, "Ultra-High-Speed Operation of Josephson Tunneling Devices," IBM J. Res. Develop. *15*, 405–407 (1971).

15. L.N. Cooper, "Bound Electron Pairs in a Degenerate Fermi Gas," Phys. Rev. *104*, 1189–90 (1956).

16. J. Bardeen, L.N. Cooper, and J.R. Schreiffer, "Microscopic Theory of Superconductivity," Phys. Rev. *106*, 162–164 (1957): "Theory of Superconductivity." See also their Nobel Price acceptance speeches in Physics Today *26*, 23–47 (July, 1973) *108*, 1175–1204 (1957).

17. T_c and H_0 taken from the Handbook of Chemistry and Physics, CRC, 1970–71 Edition. 2Δ from R. Meservey and B.B. Schwartz, Chapter 3, "Superconductivity", R.D. Parks editor, Marcel Dekker, Inc., New York (1969).

18. B.S. Deaver, Jr. and W.M. Fairbank, "Experimental Evidence for Quantized Flux in Superconducting Cylinders," Phys. Rev. Lett. 7, 43–46 (1961); R. Doll and M. Näbauer, " Experimental Proof of Magnetic Flux Quantization in a Superconducting Ring," ibid 7, 51–52 (1961).

19. F. London, *Superfluids 1*, 152, John Wiley & Sons, New York (1950).

20 K. Schwidtal and R.D. Finnegan, "Barrier-Thickness Dependence of the DC Quantum Interference Effect in Thin-Film Lead Josephson Junctions," J. Appl. Phys. *40*, 2121–2127 (1969).

21. B.D. Josephson, "Possible New Effects in Superconductive Tunneling," Phys. Letters *1*, 251–253 (1962).

22. P.W. Anderson and J.M. Rowell, "Probable Observation of the Josephson Superconductive Tunneling Effect," Phys. Rev. Lett. *10*, 230–232 (1963).

23. V. Ambegaokar and A. Baratoff, "Tunneling between Superconductors," ibid *10*, 486–489 (1963).

24. B.D. Josephson, "Coupled Superconductors," Rev. Mod. Phys. *36*, 216–220 (1964); "Supercurrents through Barriers," Advan. Phys. *14*, 419–451 (1965).

25. W. Schroen and J.P. Pritchard, Jr., "Maximum Tunneling Supercurrents through Josephson Barriers," J. Appl. Phys. *40*, 2118–2122 (1969).

26.   P.W. Anderson, "How Josephson Discovered His Effect," Phys. Today, *23*,
       23–29, (November 1970). See also T.A. Fulton, R.C. Dynes, and P.W.
       Anderson, "The Flux Shuttle — a Josephson Junction Shift Register
       Employing Single Flux Quanta," Proc. IEEE *61*, 28–35 (1973).

27.   R.C. Jaklevic, J. Lambe, A.H. Silver and J.E. Mercereau, "Quantum Inter-
       ference Effects in Josephson Tunneling," Phys. Rev. Lett. *12*, 159–160
       (1964); Macroscopic Quantum Interference in Superconductors, Phys.
       Rev. *140*, A 1628 — A 1637 (1965).

28.   J. Matisoo, "Tunneling Cryotron Flip-Flop," J. Appl. Phys. *39* 2587 (1968).

29.   J.E. Mercereau, "Quantum Engineering," in M.H. Cohen, Ed. *Supercon-
       ductivity in Science and Technology*, Chicago University Press, Chicago,
       1968.

PROBLEMS

5.1 The magnitudes of illustrative examples in Chapters 3 and 5
assumed dimensions of the order of 1μm. The result is that the
smallest unit of energy storage is three orders of magnitude smaller
for superconductors than for magnetic bubbles.

What are the comparative values if all dimensions in both examples
are scaled down by a factor of five? Are any of the required material
parameters obviously unreasonable?

5.2 Consider the stored energy of Eq. (5-11) from the point of
view of a circulating current i in an inductance L, calculating the inductance as that of a length of parallel plate transmission line of
dimensions ℓ, w and d*

a.   What current corresponds to storing one fluxoid?

b.   What is this value for the dimensions of the example below Eq.
      (5-11)?

c.   If this current has to pass through a Josephson junction of
      0.5μm^2 area, what is the required current density?

5.3 The magnitudes of the parameters assumed in problems 5-2 increase the value of j_0 by a factor of 220 from that assumed below Eq. (5-22).

a.   What is the corresponding value of λ_J.

b.   Is the assumed 0.5μm^2 junction still a "small" junction by the
      criterion of Eq. (5-22)?

5.4 Consider the circuit of Fig. 5-1, with Josephson junctions in branches 1 and 2, each with I-V characteristics given by Fig. 5-4. Current flows initially in branch 1 only.

a.   What is a simple equivalent circuit just after a gating pulse has been applied to branch 1 to switch the junction to its quasi-particle tunneling state? (ref. 13)

b.   What is the transfer time Δt for most of the current to transfer from branch 1 to branch 2?

c.   What is the value of Δt if the loop in Fig. 5-1 is a strip line of dimensions given below Eq. (5-11) both ends of the stripline being terminated by Pb-PbO-Pb Josephson junctions with $i_0 \cong 1$ milliampere.

Epilogue

The data processing technologies discussed in this book have progressed from the old to the new, from the known to the unknown, from magnetic and semiconductor to optical and superconducting technologies. These sequences should not be interpreted as implying that the new will necessarily displace the old. The old technologies are deeply entrenched and have some very attractive features on which the new technologies are advancing also, and still at a rapid rate. The advances are not solely miniaturization, but also new concepts such as magnetic bubbles, charge coupled devices, and non-volatile MNOSFET memories. Can the new technologies make an impact?

Only future events will give a clear answer. However, the reader is presented with the positive features of the new technologies along with their problems and the state of the art of the older technologies. Thus he is given a comparative base on which he can make his own judgements and decisions.

Answers to Problems

ANSWERS, Chapter 1

1.1 In the center of the chip the heat flow can be assumed entirely vertical through the $400\,\mu$m thick chip. The heat flow density in the 1 picojoule circuit case is

$$\frac{Q}{A} = \frac{1 \times 10^{-12}}{100 \times 10^{-12}} \; \times \; \frac{0.1}{10^{-6}} = 10^3 \; \text{watts/cm}^2$$

The temperature rise is

$$\Delta T = \frac{Qt}{KA} = \frac{10^3 \times .04}{1.2} = 33°\text{C}$$

The other cases would be 33,000°C! and .033°C with the approximations in the problem.

1.2 10,000, 10, and 0.11 watts respectively. There are 10^4 circuits on the chip.

1.3 30 picoseconds (comparable to the 100 picoseconds assumed for a switching event).

1.4 a.   10 and 5 milliseconds respectively

   b.   20 milliseconds

   c.   20 milliseconds

   d.   200 microseconds

   e.   10 cm by 10 cm square

1.5   500, 0.5 and 5 x 10^{-4} degrees C.

ANSWERS, Chapter 2

2.1 a.
$$C = \frac{\epsilon \epsilon_0 A}{d}$$

$$R = \frac{\varrho d}{A}$$

b. $\tau = RC = \varrho \epsilon \epsilon_0$; $\epsilon \epsilon_0 = 10^{-12}$ coulomb volt cm (10^{-10} coulomb volt meter)

For $\tau = 1$, $\varrho = 10^{12}$ ohms/cm³

For $\tau = 2.6$ x 10^5, $\varrho = 2.6$ x 10^{17}

c. $\sigma = \varrho^{-1} = Ne\mu$; $e = 1.6$ x 10^{-19} coulombs

For $\varrho = 10^{12}$, $\mu = 500 \rightarrow N = 1.25$ x 10^4/cm³

For $\varrho = 10^{12}$, $\mu = 0.5 \rightarrow N = 1.25$ x 10^7/cm³

For $\varrho = 2.6$ x 10^{17}, $\mu = 500 \rightarrow N = 4.8$ x 10^{-2}/cm³

For $\varrho = 2.6$ x 10^{17}, $\mu = 0.5 \rightarrow N = 48$/cm³

2.2 a. $10^{15} = e^{E/kT}$

$$15 = \frac{E}{kT} \log_{10}(e) = 0.433 \frac{E}{kT}$$

$\frac{E}{kT} = 34.6$, $k = 1.38$ x 10^{-23} joule degree^{-1} V = 0.9 volts
(compare 1.12 volt energy gap for silicon)

b. The time constant would be increased by a factor of 10^{15} (3.9-1) if the same model held.

2.3 Reasonable parameters (Hower et al) are $\epsilon \epsilon_0 = 1.06$ x 10^{-12} $\bar{v}$ (corresponding to v_s) = 10^7 cm/sec., = 6400 cm²/Vsec., whence

a. $N = \dfrac{2\epsilon\,\epsilon_0 v_s L}{\mu e d^2}$ scales from Si in the ratio

   $\dfrac{1.06 \times 500}{6400}$, giving the value 5×10^{15}

b. $P_v = N e v_s^2 / \mu$ scales as $\dfrac{N}{\mu}$, i.e., $\left(\dfrac{0.5}{6} \times \dfrac{500}{6400},\right)$ giving a value

   $1.6 \times 10^{-3}\ (.065) \approx 10^{-4}$ watts/μm^3

c.   10 picoseconds

d.   0.02 picojoules

2.4   a. $e^x = 1 + x = .9996,\ x = .0004;$

   $e^{nx} = 1 + nx = 1 - 256 \times .004 \doteq .90 = 90\%$

b. $e^{128y} = 2,\quad 128y = 1n2 = .693,\ y = .0054$

   $e^{-y} = 1 - .0054 = 0.9946 = 99.46\%$

c.   By launching a finite amount of charge, q (0) for every zero
   bit, when a "1" charge is transferred to a prior "0" location,
   some of the charge lost in the transfer is compensated by pick-
   ing up the residual "0" charge.

2.5

$$\exp\left(-\dfrac{0.36e}{kT}\right) = .5, \quad \dfrac{0.36e}{kT} = 1n\,2 = .693$$

$kT = 0.52e;\ 1eV = 11{,}605.8^\circ K,\ T = 6{,}050^\circ K.$

ANSWERS, Chapter 3
3.1

a.

Material	a(A°)	T_c	A (ergs/cm)
Fe	2.87	1043	5.0×10^{-6}
Co	3.54	1403	5.5×10^{-6}

b. 6.1×10^{-7}

Note that for more dilute magnetic materials — such as magnetic oxides — A decreases more rapidly than a increases, resulting in lower values of T_c. When T_c is below room temperature the material is not useful for many applications. Hence the conclusion of Eq. (3-13)

3.2 $kT = 1.38 \times 10^{-16} \times 300 = 4.14 \times 10^{-14}$ ergs $= 4.14 \times 10^{-9}$ picojoules

$E/kT = 10^5$, can reduce E by 1,000 and maintain $E/kT > 100$

3.3 a. $N = 6 \times 10^{16}/cm^3$; $e = 4.8 \times 10^{-10}$, $\ell = 10^{-4}$, $Ne\ell = 290$

$M_s = 45$, $4\Pi M_s = 570$

b. v_s (FET) $= 10^7$ cm/sec; $- v_s$ (bubbles) $= 2 \times 10^3$ cm/sec
$$\text{ratio} = 500$$

c. μ (FET) $= 500 \times 300 = 1.5 \times 10^5$ cm/sec/esu

μ (bubbles) $= 1,000$ cm/sec/emu
$$\text{ratio} = 150$$

d.   In comparing FET's and magnetic bubbles, the polarization factors in the two cases are comparable. The 500-fold higher v_s value for the FET accounts for its higher speed, but the 150 fold higher μ value largely cancels the power dissipation price (v_s/μ) per unit volume.

The main reason for the larger FET $P\tau$ product is its larger volume; i.e., further semiconductor miniaturization, if feasible, could lead to further improvements in $P\tau$ products.

3.4 a. $E = E_0 \, e^{-\alpha x} \sin^2 Fx$

$$\frac{dE}{dx} = 0 \rightarrow \tan Fx = \frac{2F}{\alpha} \qquad x = 2°C^{-1} = .053 \, \mu m$$

b. $E_0 = 100 \, h\nu = \dfrac{100 \times 1.987 \times 10^{-8}}{6300}$ ergs $= 3.15 \times 10^{-10}$ ergs

$e^{-\alpha x} \sin^2 Fx = e^{-2} \sin^2 (2.84°) = \left(\dfrac{1}{7.4}\right) (.0946)^2 = 3.43 \times 10^{-4}$

$E = 3.15 \times 10^{-10}/3.43 \times 10^{-4} = 0.92 \times 10^{-6}$ ergs $= .09$ picojoules

c. $E_k = (1 - e^{-2}) \times 200 \times .035 \times 10^{-12}$ joules = 9.2 picojoules

(note: c is very much an underestimate as an appreciable thickness of the substrate supporting the film also would be heated by conduction from the film)

ANSWERS, Chapter 4

4.1 a. $\tan \theta_m = 1/32$

compare to $\sin \theta_1 = \dfrac{1}{4}$

The lens would intercept the zeroth order only and the "image" would be a uniform gray exposure.

b. For F(1), $\tan \theta_{max} = 1/3.2$ $\theta_{max} = 17.4°$ whereas $\sin \theta_1 = 0.25$,

$\theta_1 = 14.5°$. The lens captures the 0 & ±1 orders. The result is an image with sinusoidal intensity variation.

4.2 a. $\dfrac{mv^2}{2} = eV$, $v^2 = \dfrac{2eV}{m} = 2 \times \dfrac{4.8 \times 10^{-10}}{9.1 \times 10^{-28}} \times \dfrac{10}{3} = \dfrac{3.2}{9.1} \times 10^{19}$

$v = 1.88 \times 10^9$ cm/sec, $\qquad t = 5.32 \times 10^{-10}$ sec.

b. $v_t = at$; $a = eE/m = \dfrac{4.8 \times 10^{-10} \times 0.2}{9.1 \times 10^{-28}}$

$a = 1.03 \times 10^{17}$ cm/sec^2, $\quad v_t = 5.5 \times 10^7$ cm/sec

c. $\dfrac{1}{2}$ $at^2 = 1.5 \times 10^{-2}$ cm

$t_{20\,cm} = 1.064 \times 10^{-8}$ sec, $v_t t_{20} = 0.59$ cm

d. $\Delta\theta = \dfrac{200\lambda}{0.5} = \dfrac{200 \times .514}{.5} \times 10^{-4} \approx .02$ radians with a deflection after a 20cm path of 0.4 cm.

4.3 a. $f = \dfrac{1}{\phi}$, $\Phi^2 = .01$, $f = 10$

b. $\Delta t = (1-\cos \Phi) \times \dfrac{10^5}{3 \times 10^{10}} = \dfrac{\Phi^2}{2} \times \dfrac{10^5}{3 \times 10^{10}} = \dfrac{.005 \times 10^5}{3 \times 10^{10}}$

t = 0.17 microseconds

Note — in single mode fibers or self-foc fibers the time delay is much less.

4.4 a. 4 picojoules

b. In ref. 17 planar technology is used such that both modulating electrodes are on the surface of a large block of Li NbO_3, applying the voltage across w rather than d. (d is also rather large in this structure, of the order of w.) w is also reduced to about $60 \mu m$, essentially only by reducing the safety factor S allowed in the spreading in the plane of the trapped light.

c. Resistive losses through the semiconductor to the junction are high. Also V_π for GaAs is several times larger than V_π for Li NbO_3.

d. $100 \times \left(\dfrac{1}{250}\right)^2 \times 1{,}000$ picojoules = 1.6 picojoules

4.5 The linear dimension of $V \cong N\lambda/2$ where N is the number of $\lambda/2$ multilayers

The number of resolution elements in 4Π radians is $4\Pi/\Delta\theta^2$

Angular resolution elements = $\dfrac{4\Pi}{\Delta\theta^2}$ = $\dfrac{\Pi^2 N}{\sqrt{2}}$ = N_θ

This means there can be N_θ reference beam directions, each recording N data points. Also approximately N wavelengths can be used. The total information is

$$N\, N^2_\theta \quad \dfrac{\pi^6 N^3}{2} \approx \dfrac{4\Pi^4 V}{\lambda^3}$$

4.6 $Re^{n\sigma L} = 1.$ $n\sigma L = Ln_e (3.33) = 1.2$

a. $n = \dfrac{1.2}{3 \times 10^{-15} \times 10^{-2}} = 4 \times 10^{16}$ per cm^3

For $\lambda = 0.9 \,\mu m$, $h\nu = \dfrac{1.98 \times 10^{-12}}{0.9}$ ergs = 2.2×10^{-19} joules

b. $P_T = (4 \times 10^{16} \times 2.2 \times 10^{-19} \times 10^3)$ picojoules = 8.8 picojoules

c. $j = \dfrac{4 \times 10^{16} \times 1.6 \times 10^{-19} \times 10^{-4}}{10^{-9}} = 480$ amperes/cm^2

ANSWERS, Chapter 5

5.1 Scaling the dimensions of magnetic example by a factor of five presumably would leave A and Q unchanged and reduce δ by 5. Other changes

K increase 25 (Eq.3-11) to 1.6×10^5 ergs/cm^3 (Eq. 3-17)

M_s increase 5 to 2850 (Eq. 3-18)

4 Π M increase 5 to 2850 (Eq. 3-18)

H_A increase 5 to 14,250 (Eq. 3-18)

Assuming no changes in μ or v_s, this would decrease E by 25 to 1.4×10^{-5} picojoules. The requisite materials parameters fall in the hexagonal ferrites area of Fig. 3-3, for example. They also fall in the range of amorphous magnetic bubbles materials.

Scaling the dimensions of the superconducting example by 5 *increases* E by 5 (Eq. 5-11) to 5×10^{-6} picojoules, *only a factor of 4 smaller than the magnetic example* if a single fluxoid is stored. The corresponding value of H is increased by a factor of 25 to 500 gauss, exceeding the critical field of tin (though not of lead or niobium). The lower limit $d^* \cong 2\lambda$ is reached by this scaling. Of course, the geometrical ratios can be changed to give different results.

5.2 a. $E = \dfrac{Li^2}{2}$ where $L = \dfrac{\mu_0 d^* \ell}{w}$

and $\mu_0 = 0.4\Pi$ picohenries/μm

Therefore, for dimensions in microns

$\dfrac{1.76 \times 10^{-6} w}{1 d^*} = 0.2\Pi\, i^2\, \dfrac{d^* \ell}{w}$

$i = 1.67 \times 10^{-3}\, \dfrac{w}{\ell d^*}$ amperes

b. For $\frac{w}{\ell} = \frac{1}{3}$, d* = 0.5, i = 1.11 milliamperes

c. 2.22 milliamperes per square micrometer — i.e., 22,000 amperes per square centimeter.

Note that this value exceeds the particular early experimental values quoted after Eq. (5-12)

5.3 a. λ_J will decrease by a factor of $\sqrt{220}$ = 14.8 to 0.34 μm.

b. $2\lambda_J = 0.68\,\mu$m is now slightly smaller than w = 0.71 μm, so that the junction is of an intermediate size.

5.4 a.

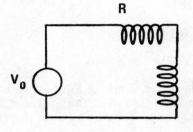

where R is very small and $V_o = 2\Delta/e$

b. $i(t) = \frac{V_o}{R}(1-\exp\frac{-(R)}{L}t) = \frac{V_o}{R}(1-1+\frac{R}{L}t)$

for transfer of a fractionally small part of $\frac{V_o}{R}$

$\therefore\ i = \frac{V_o\Delta t}{L}, \quad \Delta t = \frac{L\Delta i}{V_o}$

c. V_o = 2.7 millivolts ⌐ ⎯ ⌐ ⸝⸝

RETURN TO: PHYSICS-ASTRONOMY LIBRARY
351 LeConte Hall

LOAN PERIOD 1 **1-MONTH**	2	3
4	5	6

ALL BOOKS MAY BE RECALLED AFTER 7 DAYS
Books may be renewed by calling 510-642-3122

DUE AS STAMPED BELOW

FORM NO. DD 22
2M 7-10

UNIVERSITY OF CALIFORNIA, BERKELEY
Berkeley, California 94720–6000